Dana Estes, Heinrich Schellen

Spectrum Analysis explained

Dana Estes, Heinrich Schellen

Spectrum Analysis explained

ISBN/EAN: 9783337139629

Printed in Europe, USA, Canada, Australia, Japan

Cover: Foto ©ninafisch / pixelio.de

More available books at **www.hansebooks.com**

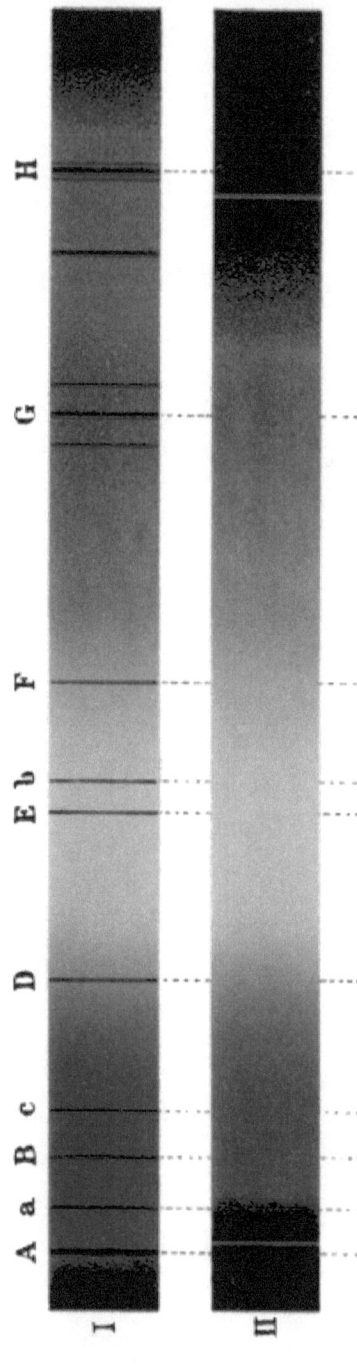

SPECTRUM ANALYSIS

EXPLAINED.

ITS USES TO SCIENCE ILLUSTRATED, SHOWING ITS APPLICATION IN MICROSCOPICAL RESEARCH, AND TO DISCOVERIES OF THE PHYSICAL CONDITION AND MOVEMENTS OF THE HEAVENLY BODIES, AND INCLUDING AN EXPLANATION OF THE RECEIVED THEORY OF

SOUND, HEAT, LIGHT, AND COLOR.

COMPILED BY THE EDITOR OF

"HALF-HOUR RECREATIONS IN POPULAR SCIENCE,"

FROM THE WORKS AND OBSERVATIONS OF

PROFS. SCHELLEN, ROSCOE, HUGGINS, LOCKYER, YOUNG, AND OTHERS.

FULLY ILLUSTRATED.

BOSTON:
ESTES AND LAURIAT,
143 WASHINGTON STREET.
1872.

Entered, according to Act of Congress, in the year 1872,
By DANA ESTES,
In the Office of the Librarian of Congress, at Washington.

Stereotyped at the Boston Stereotype Foundry,
19 Spring Lane.

4. Spectrum Analysis Explained, and its Uses to Science Illustrated.

Introductory.

THIS work is founded upon a series of lectures delivered by the author during the winter of 1869, before the "Society for Scientific Lectures," in Cologne. Its object is, on the one hand, to give a clear and familiar representation of the nature and phenomena of spectrum analysis, enabling an educated person not previously familiar with physical science to become acquainted with the newest and most brilliant discovery of this century; and, on the other hand, to show the important position which spectrum analysis has acquired in the pursuit of physics, chemistry, technology, physiology, and astronomy, as well as its adaptability to almost every kind of scientific investigation.

The general reader will be introduced by this book into a new realm of science, the dominion of which has extended in a few years over all terrestrial substances, and even beyond them to the most distant parts of the universe. He will learn to decipher the new language of *light*, which by unequivocal signs yields him information not only concerning the nature of terrestrial substances, but also of the physical constitution of the heavenly bodies.

To facilitate the due appreciation of the results which have been obtained by the application of spectrum analysis to the heavenly bodies, the author has given with each class of objects a summary of the information hitherto furnished by the telescope, and has sought to give a glance in passing at the progressive development and partial transformation of the heavenly bodies.

The author acknowledges with grateful thanks the valuable assistance rendered him by various scientific men who have kindly communicated to him the results of their labors, among whom he would especially mention Messrs. Huggins, Secchi, Lockyer, Zöllner, Janssen, Morton, and Young.

On the Artificial Sources of High Degrees of Heat and Light.

The total eclipse of the sun in India of the 18th of August, 1868, was an event which, it will be remembered, excited extreme interest in the scientific world, and led to a large expenditure of money and labor, in order that a new method of investigation — spectrum analysis — might be applied to those mysterious phenomena invariably present at a total solar eclipse, the nature and character of which the unassisted powers of the telescope had proved themselves inadequate to reveal. The brilliant results obtained at this eclipse were fully confirmed by the more recent observations made in North America during the total eclipse of the 7th of August, 1869, and the records of those eclipses laid before the various scientific societies clearly assert the triumph of spectrum analysis. On this account, the new method of investigation has excited great interest in all cultivated circles, and therefore a familiar and comprehensive exposition of the details of spectrum analysis, in which is shown the great value of this method of research in every department of physical science, seems not uncalled for.

By *spectrum* is not understood in physics a spectre or ghostly apparition, as the verbal interpretation of the word might well lead one to suppose, but that beautiful image, brilliant with all the colors of the rainbow, which is obtained when the light of the sun, or any other brilliant object, is allowed to pass through a triangular piece of glass — a prism.

The unassisted eye can perceive no difference in the light from the heavenly bodies and that from various artificial sources, beyond a variation in color and brilliancy; but it is quite otherwise when the light is viewed through a prism. There are then formed very beautiful colored images or spectra, the constitution and appearance of which depend upon the nature of the substance emitting the light. The different appearances presented by these colored images are so entirely characteristic, that to every substance, when luminous in a gaseous form, there corresponds a peculiar spectrum, which belongs only to that particular substance.

It follows, therefore, that when the spectra of different substances have been determined once for all, by previous researches, and have been recorded in maps or impressed upon the memory, it is easy in any future investigation to recognize at once, from the form of the spectrum which a body of unknown constitution presents, the individual substances of which it is composed.

This statement presents in general terms the nature of spectrum analysis. It *analyzes* bodies into their constituent parts, not as the chemist, with alembics and retorts, with re-agents and precipitates, but by means of the spectra which these substances give when in a state of intense luminosity.

Spectrum analysis in no way supplants the methods of chemical analysis hitherto in use; for its function is neither to decompose nor to combine bodies, but rather to reconnoitre an unknown territory, and to stand sentinel, and signalize to the physicist, the chemist, and the astronomer, the presence of any substance brought beneath its scrutiny.

With what acuteness, with what delicacy does spectrum analysis accomplish this task! When the balance, the microscope, and every other means of research at the command of the physicist and the chemist utterly fail, one look in the spectroscope is sufficient, in most cases, to reveal the presence of a substance. If a pound of common salt be divided into 500,000 equal parts, the weight of one of these portions is called a milligramme. The chemist is able, by the use of the most delicate scales and the application of special skill, to determine the weight of such a particle; but in doing so, he comes close upon the limits of his power of detecting by chemical means the presence of sodium, the chief element in common salt. But if that small milligramme be subdivided into three million parts, we arrive at so minute a particle that all power of discerning it fails, and yet even this excessively small quantity is sufficient to be recognized with certainty in a spectroscope. We have but to strike together the pages of an old dusty book in order to perceive immediately in a spectroscope placed at some distance, the flash of a line of yellow light which we shall presently learn is an unfailing sign of the presence of sodium.

It was to be expected that so sensitive a means of investigation, from which no known substance can escape, would very soon lead to the tracking out and discovery of new elements which, till then, had remained unknown, either because they are scattered very sparingly in nature, or stand out with so little that is characteristic, from some other substances, that the imperfect chemical methods hitherto in use have not been able to distinguish them.

This expectation was brilliantly realized even by the first steps taken in this direction. The two Heidelberg professors, Bunsen and Kirchhoff, to whom we are indebted for the discovery of spectrum analysis and its application to practical science, very soon discovered with their new instrument, two new metals, Cæsium and Rubidium, to which two others, Thallium and Indium, have been since added.

But all the brilliant and astounding results which spectrum analysis has furnished in the provinces of physics and chemistry have been far surpassed by its performances in that of astronomy. Newton's law of gravitation has given us the means of calculating the courses of the heavenly bodies, of projecting the orbits of the earth, the planets and comets, and of predicting their relative positions in these orbits, together with the accompanying phenomena of the ebb and flow of the tides, and the eclipses and occultations of the heavenly bodies. But this same gravitation chains man to the earth, and forbids him to leave it. It is therefore only on the wings of light, that news reaches him of the existence of those numberless worlds by which he is surrounded. The light alone, which proceeds from these stars, is the winged messenger which can bring him information of their being and nature; spectrum analysis has made this light into a ladder on which the human mind can rise billions and billions of miles, far into immeasurable space, in order to investigate the chemical constitution of the stars, and study their physical conditions.

Until within a few years, the telescope was the only means by which these investigations could be carried on, and the intelligence derived from this source concerning the stars and nebulæ was very scant, being confined to but partial information of their outward form, size, and color.

Since the year 1859, spectrum analysis has entered the service of astronomy, and its performances for the short space of eleven years are, in the most widely-differing ways, *perfectly astounding*.

It is possible by means of a prism to decompose into its component parts the light of the sun, the planets, the fixed stars, comets and nebulæ, and thus obtain their spectra in the same way as that of earthly luminous substances. By a careful comparison of the spectra of the stars with the well-known spectra of terrestrial substances, it can be determined, from their complete agreement or disagreement, with a certainty almost amounting to mathematical precision, whether these substances do or do not exist in those remote heavenly bodies.

The foregoing statements present, in general terms, the essence and scope of spectrum analysis. Its starting-point is the spectrum of each individual substance, and in order to obtain this it is requisite that the substance should not only be luminous, but should emit a *sufficient quantity* of light. Dark bodies are not available for spectrum analysis;

if they are to be submitted to its scrutiny, they must first be brought into a state of vivid luminosity.

That the nature of the analysis of light may be more easily understood, we will first proceed to explain

The Solar Spectrum.

If a ray of sunshine be allowed to pass through a small, round hole in the window-shutter of a darkened room, as is shown in Fig. I., there will appear a round, white spot of light exactly in the direction of the ray, upon a screen placed opposite the opening, as will be seen indicated by the dotted lines in the figure. A very different appearance will be presented if the ray of light be made to fall upon a prism. The ray is at once deflected from its straight course upwards, that is to say, towards the base of the prism, and away from the sharp edge of the refracting surfaces, which, as represented in the drawing, are turned downwards: on its emergence from the prism it no longer remains one single ray, as it entered the window-shutter, but is separated into very many single-colored rays, which, as they continue to diverge, form upon the screen an elongated band of brilliant colors, instead of the former round, white image of the sun. In this brilliant band the individual colors blend gradually one into the other, beginning at that end lying nearest the direction of the incident ray (the lowest end in the figure), with the least refrangible color, a dark and very beautiful red; this passes imperceptibly into orange, and orange again into bright yellow; a pure green succeeds, which is shaded off into a brilliant blue, and this gives place to a rich, deep indigo; a delicate purple leads finally to a soft violet, by which the range of the visible rays is terminated. (A faint picture of this magnificent solar image is given in No. 1 of the Frontispiece; this is called the *spectrum*.) In the above-mentioned colors of the solar spectrum, the eye discerns numberless gradations, which pass imperceptibly from one to another; and since language does not suffice to give separate names to each of these, we must content ourselves with designating only the seven principal groups, which are known as the colors of the spectrum.

This experiment furnishes conclusive evidence that white

Fig. I.

EXHIBITION OF THE SOLAR SPECTRUM.

light is not simple and indivisible, but composed of innumerable colored rays, each of which possesses its own peculiar degree of refrangibility, and therefore, on refraction, pursues a separate path. The prism analyzes white light; the result is the separation of all the colored rays of which it is composed, and the consequent formation of the colored image called the *spectrum*.

The decomposition of sunlight by refraction is shown in various phenomena known to the ancients as well as ourselves, though they were not able, as we are, to trace them back to their true cause. The rainbow, with its pure but delicate colors, the sparkle of the cut jewel in its brilliant flashes, the play of color emitted by cut glass, and the prismatic facets of crystal lustres as the sun shines upon them, the glow of the clouds and high mountain peaks in the various colored light of the rising and setting sun, — all these effects are occasioned by the decomposition of white light by its refraction on passing through glass in a prismatic form, through drops of liquid, or through vapor.

The colors of the solar spectrum possess a purity and brilliancy to be met with nowhere else; they are all perfectly indivisible, and cannot be further decomposed, as may be easily proved on attempting to analyze a colored ray by means of a second prism. If a small, round hole be made in the screen in any portion of the image of the spectrum, — the extreme red, for instance (Fig. I.), — a red ray passes through it, and appears upon the opposite wall as a round spot of red light, precisely in the same direction as the red rays left the prism on the other side of the screen. If a second prism be interposed in the path of the ray that has passed through the screen, the ray will suffer a second refraction, and the image be thrown upon another place (higher up in the figure) on the wall; this new image, however, is simply red, like the incident ray, and by a careful adjustment of the prism shows no elongation, but appears perfectly round.

This decomposition of sunlight, or white light, as it is usually termed, is called dispersion, and is caused by refraction, by which is meant the deviation of a ray of light from a straight line when it strikes any transparent substance (as, for instance, glass or water) obliquely. Different colors are said to have different degrees of refrangibility; and by this we mean, that different colored rays of light, being passed through a triangular piece of glass, or prism, are turned more or less from the direction in which they entered it. Thus the colors of the rainbow have each a different degree of refrangibility, from red, which has the least, to violet, which has the greatest; and when white light, which is composed of all these colors combined, is analyzed, or separated, these colors are refracted, or turned at different angles, so as to separate, though each is beautifully blended with the one next it. The same is true of light from any source. It is only necessary that any substance should be made sufficiently luminous, to become thoroughly sifted, or analyzed, by means of the spectroscope.

We will now proceed to explain how all substances, such as gases, metals, earths, etc., may be made sufficiently luminous to be made available for spectrum analyses. It is necessary to have sufficient heat to volatilize or turn into vapor any substance to be analyzed. For this purpose many ingenious contrivances have been invented, one of which was invented by Bunsen, one of the discoverers of spectrum analysis. This is called the Bunsen burner, and consists of a gas burner, arranged with a chamber beneath it, where atmospheric air is mixed with the gas before passing up the tube to feed the burner. The flame from this burner is non-luminous, but its heat is intense, and may be made much greater if the atmospheric air, instead of being left to mix itself with the gas, be forced in by means of a powerful blowpipe.

In the Bunsen burner, the combustion of coal gas ensues slowly and incompletely; slowly, because the hydrogen in combination with carbon is supplied only in small quantities; incompletely, because the gases are not mixed in due proportions, and the nitrogen of the air presents a hinderance. If, on the contrary, pure hydrogen gas be previously mixed with as much pure oxygen as will insure its complete combustion (two volumes of hydrogen with one of oxygen), oxyhydrogen gas is obtained, which, when ignited, explodes with a fearful noise, and occasions sometimes the destruction of the strongest vessels. The heat evolved by this combustion is the greatest which can at present be produced by *chemical* means, and it is sufficient to accomplish the fusion of substances which have borne unchanged the action of the hottest furnaces.

In order to make the oxyhydrogen flame a source of intense light, a cylinder of well-burnt lime is placed upon the socket of the lamp, and the flame directed against the upper part. It begins at once to glow, and soon throws out a dazzling, incandescent, or white-heat light. This is called the oxyhydrogen or Drummond's lime-light.

The Electric Spark.

To attain, however, the greatest amount of heat and light which can at present be produced, we must leave the province of chemistry, with its processes of combustion, and turn to that of electricity, where we are encountered by a host of phenomena, accompanied by an intense degree of light and heat.

Besides the well-known machines which excite electricity through the friction of a glass disk, there has been added of late a contrivance called an induction machine, which yields a rich supply of electric force, and gives a spark of intense brilliancy. In all electrical motors arranged for exhibiting light, sparks are formed between two metallic poles or pieces of wire, which are placed in contact with those parts of the machine which collect the positive and negative electricity. By the mutual attraction of the two electricities, and the struggle for union, there ensues a tension of electricity at the end of the metal poles when they are separated from each other; if this be so strong that the obstacle presented by the stratum of air between the metallic conductors is overcome by it, then the electricities are instantly united, and the union takes place in that form of light and heat which is called the *electric spark*.

The amount of heat thus generated depends upon the degree of tension and the quantities of electricity by the union of which it is produced; but in most cases it is so great that small particles of the metal poles are volatilized, and become luminous. The glowing metallic vapor affects the color of the spark, which therefore appears with various kinds of light, according to the nature of the conductors. These phenomena afford us, in aid of our researches with spectrum analysis, a very simple method of volatilizing and raising to a high degree of luminosity most of the metals, and other substances which are conductors of electricity. To obtain the same result with liquids, it is only necessary to place one of the metal poles in the liquid to be examined, and to bring the other sufficiently near the surface for the spark to pass from it to the liquid. By the heat of the spark a small portion of the liquid is volatilized and made luminous.

THE VOLTAIC ARC.

It will be well now to turn our attention for a short time to that source of electricity which is able to evolve the highest degree of heat with the most intense light — namely, the voltaic arc, or the electric light. When the poles of a powerful voltaic battery of fifty or sixty elements are connected, by means of two metal wires, with two pieces of carbon, a, b (Fig. II.), and these brought into contact, the electricity generated by the battery is discharged between them through the carbon, which is nearly as good a conductor as the metal. If these pieces of carbon be pointed at the ends, an extraordinarily intense light is emitted on the passage of the current at the points of contact, and they may be separated one or two tenths of an inch without interrupting the discharge. The apparatus is then placed in the lantern,

Fig. II.

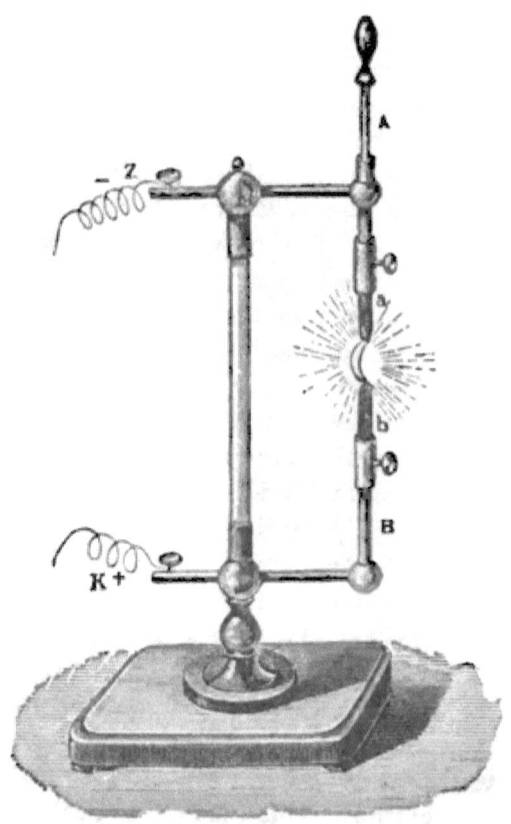

THE ELECTRIC LIGHT.

which is provided with requisite arrangements to keep the carbon points at a proper distance from each other, and also with a small mirror and lens to project the light through a slit in the lantern. The complete arrangement is called

The Electric Lamp.

To exhibit the spectrum, the room should be darkened, and the electric lamp placed on a table, with the wires connected with a battery. (See Fig. III.) The light from the

SPECTRUM ANALYSIS EXPLAINED.

Fig. III.

THE ELECTRIC LAMP.

carbon points passes through the narrow, vertical slit in the lamp, and by means of the movable lens. D. a distinct image of the slit is thrown through the prisms E E upon a screen at a distance of about twelve feet, and we behold a magnificent spectrum, about three feet long and sixteen inches wide, exhibiting the whole range of colors, as shown in No. 1 of the Frontispiece, with this difference. In No. 1, Frontispiece, the colors are crossed with dark lines, this being a feature of the Solar Spectrum which will be explained farther on. The colors from the *incandescent* or white-hot carbon points succeed each other without the slightest interruption. Their limits are not sharply defined; they rather blend gradually one into the other, and thus form an unbroken or *continuous* spectrum.

Recombination of the Colors of the Spectrum.

If white light be actually composed of the colors contained in the spectrum, then the recombination of the same colors must reproduce white light. The simplest method of collecting several rays of light into one point is by a convex lens or a burning-glass. If the sun's rays fall perpendicularly on such a glass, the refraction they suffer in their passage through it causes them to converge to one point — the focus. To accomplish by this means the recombination of the colored rays of the spectrum of the electric light, a cylindrical lens must be interposed between the prism and the screen on which the spectrum of the small line of light issuing from the slit is extended to a length of some six feet: this lens is a convex lens of peculiar form, which possesses the property of recombining in a point all the rays issuing from each point of the line of light passing through the slit after dispersion by the prism, and therefore of representing the whole of the rays of that short line of light again as a small line. When, therefore, this lens is placed at a proper distance behind the prism, the colors of the spectrum disappear from the screen, and are replaced by a short line of light, in which all the colored rays issuing from the prism have been recombined, and the white light reproduced out of which they originated.

The Continuous Spectra of Solid and Liquid Bodies.

When the carbon points used for the production of the electric light are carefully prepared, and completely free from all extraneous substances, the light is purely white, being emitted exclusively by solid particles of carbon in a state of incandescence. The spectrum of this light is, therefore, continuous, like that of incandescent lime; it is unbroken by gaps in the colors, or by sudden transitions from one color to another, and is uninterrupted by either dark or bright bands.

All other *incandescent* bodies, whether solid or liquid, give a similar spectrum, the colors being distributed in the order represented in the Frontispiece, No. 1. If, instead of the lime-light, the magnesium light, the light of an incandescent platinum wire, or the flame of coal gas in which light is produced by incandescent particles of carbon, be analyzed by the prism, continuous spectra are always obtained, but with this difference, that the various groups of color are not always distributed in exactly the same proportion in each individual spectrum; and therefore, according to the kind of light employed, sometimes red, sometimes yellow, and sometimes violet predominates. Therefore, where there is *a continuous spectrum without gaps, and containing every shade of color, the light is derived from an incandescent solid or liquid body.*

The Spectra of Vapors and Gases.

Very different spectra are obtained when the source of light is not an incandescent *solid* or *liquid* body, but a *vapor* or a *gas* in a glowing state. Instead of a continuous succession of colors, the spectrum then exhibits a series of distinct bright-colored bands, separated one from another by dark spaces.

The characteristic feature of spectra obtained from luminous vapors or gases is the want of continuity in the succession of the colors. Such a spectrum is composed of distinct colored bands, irregularly arranged, with dark spaces between them, and is therefore called a *discontinuous spectrum*, a *spectrum of bright lines*, or a *gas spectrum*.

The spectra of the vapors of potassium, sodium, cæsium, and rubidium are represented in Nos. 2, 3, 4, and 5 of the Frontispiece.

The colored plate at the beginning shows certain spectra, observed by means of the spectroscope. It contains five specimens of discontinuous or gas spectrums. Fig. I. represents the solar spectrum, which is, as we showed before, simple white light, or sunlight analyzed into its constituent parts. Fig. II. shows the spectrum of potassium. It is continuous, with the exception of the line in the extreme red, and another in the extreme violet, and without these two lines, would show the spectrum of an incandescent solid or liquid body, or, in other words, a body raised to the point of white heat. Fig. III. shows the spectrum of sodium or salt. This spectrum contains neither red, orange, green, blue, nor violet. It is marked by a very brilliant yellow ray. Of all metals, sodium is that which possesses the greatest spectral sensibility. In fact, it has been ascertained that *one two-hundred millionth of a grain of salt* is enough to cause the appearance of the yellow line of sodium. A very little dust scattered in the room is enough to produce it: a circumstance which shows how abundantly sodium is scattered throughout nature. Kirchhoff has also ascertained that it exists in the sun and the fixed stars.

Figures IV. and V. show the spectra of *cæsium* and rubidium, metals discovered by Bunsen and Kirchhoff, by means of Spectrum Analysis. The former is distinguished by two blue lines, the latter by two brilliant red lines, and two less intense violet lines.

SPECTRUM ANALYSIS EXPLAINED.

Two other metals, *thallium* and *indium*, have lately been discovered by other scientists by the same means.

Terrestrial substances must be volatilized, or made into vapor, to be examined. The spectra of incandescent *solid* and *liquid* bodies are *continuous*, and resemble each other so closely, that only in a very few instances can they be distinguished; spectra of this kind are, therefore, not suitable for the recognition of a substance, though they authorize the conclusion, as a rule, that the substance is either in a solid or liquid state. Only the discontinuous spectra, consisting of colored lines which are obtained from a gas or vapor, are sufficiently characteristic to enable the observer to pronounce with certainty, by the number, position, and relative brightness of these lines, the chemical constitution of the vapors by which the light has been emitted. It follows from this circumstance that spectrum analysis deals pre-eminently with the investigation of *gas spectra*, and that for the examination of a substance which does not exist in nature in the form of gas or vapor, the first step must be to place it in this condition. We explained how this is done by the use of the Electric Lamp and the Drummond Lime-light.

LIGHT.

Although the theory of light is now so completely understood that we are able to explain the most complicated optical phenomena, yet an elementary reply to the question, What is the nature of light? still presents some difficulty. We perceive the operation of this power of nature in all directions, and in the most manifold ways; the sun, as it stands in full splendor in the heavens, pours forth but a single tone of color over the earth, and yet the individual objects in the landscape appear in the most varied and glorious tints. What then are these colors? How are they developed out of the white light which the sun and other luminous bodies emit?

We need not seek to avoid answering this question, if we can succeed in giving a clear insight into the phenomena of spectrum analysis; for we have already intimated that the world of color is the peculiar province of this new method of investigation.

The approaches to science are frequently obstructed by strange propositions, discouraging and apparently contradictory, which seem to the uninitiated like those ghosts that haunted the way by which Dante and his heavenly guide descended to the realms of the departed; with a little courage, however, we may easily traverse this dreaded path, seize hold of the harmless apparitions, and make friends first with one and then with another as we approach them.

We will therefore boldly grasp the proposed inquiry; if the answer to it cannot be exhaustive, it will at least contain material enough to incite to further reflection, and perhaps also afford the necessary basis for a more easy comprehension of the elaborate theories which are enunciated in physical treatises.

According to the theory generally received at present, the whole universe is an immeasurable sea of highly attenuated matter, imperceptible to the senses, in which the heavenly bodies move with scarcely any impediment. This fluid, which is called *ether*, fills the whole of space — fills the intervals between the heavenly bodies, as well as the pores or interstices between the atoms of a substance. The smallest particles of this subtle matter are in constant vibratory motion; when this motion is communicated to the retina of the eye, it produces, if the impression upon the nerves be sufficiently strong, a sensation which we call *light*.

Every substance, therefore, which sets the ether in powerful vibration, is luminous; strong vibrations are perceived as intense light, and weak vibrations as faint light, but both of them proceed from the luminous object at the extraordinary speed of 186,000 miles in a second, and they necessarily diminish in strength in proportion as they spread themselves over a greater space.

Light is not therefore a separate substance, but only the vibration of a substance, which, according to its various forms of motion, generates light, heat, or electricity.

Analogy between Light and Sound.

This representation of the nature of light ceases to be surprising when we come to compare the vibrations of ether with those of atmospheric air, and draw a parallel between light and sound — between the eye and the ear.

A string set in vibration causes a compression and rarefaction of the surrounding air; in front of it the air is pushed together and condensed; behind it the vacuum it creates is filled up by the surrounding air, which thus becomes rarefied for the moment. This periodic movement of the air is transmitted to our ears at the rate of about 1,100 feet in a second; it strikes against the tympanum, and occasions, by its further impulse on the auditory nerves and brain, the sensation we call *sound*. Air in motion, by its influence on the organs of hearing, is the cause of sound; ether in motion, by its influence on the organs of sight, is the cause of light. Without air, or some other medium whereby the vibration of bodies can be propagated to our ears, no sound is possible. As a sonorous body throws off no actual substance of sound, but only occasions a vibration of the air, *so a luminous body sends out no substance of light, but only gives an impulse to the ether, and sets it in vibration.*

A musical sound, in contradistinction to mere noise, is produced only when the impulses of the air reach the ear at regular intervals; if the intervals between the impulses are not sufficiently regular, the ear is only conscious of a hissing, a rushing, or a humming noise; a musical sound requires perfect regularity in the succession of impulses.

The pitch of a musical note depends on the number of

impulses in a given time — as, for instance, in a second; the greater the number of vibrations in a second, the higher will be the note produced. When the single impulses are fewer than sixteen or more than forty thousand in a second, the ear is no longer sensible of a musical sound: in the first case, it either perceives only an undefined, deep hum, or else it distinguishes the individual strokes upon the tympanum, and becomes sensible of them as distinct blows; in the latter case, there is an impression of a sharp, but equally indefinite shrill or hissing noise. The limits of susceptibility of the ear for musical sounds lie between sixteen and forty thousand impulses per second. The number of vibrations in a second given by a normal tuning-fork was determined in the year 1859 to be 435 in a temperature of 15° C. (59° F.)*

The truth of the foregoing statements may be easily proved in the following manner. A disk of zinc is fastened to an axis which can be set in rapid rotation by means of a cord working over a large wheel. The disk is perforated with eight series of holes, placed along eight concentric circles; the holes are of the same size in each circle, and at equal distances from each other, so that their number increases in each ring from the centre to the edge.

When the disk, by means of the large wheel, is set in uniform motion at the rate of one revolution in a second, and one circle of the holes is blown upon with considerable force through a glass or metal tube, a note is heard: by blowing upon the next series higher, the note is of a higher pitch; a lower set of holes gives, on the contrary, a deeper note; so that if all the rings were blown upon in succession, from the

---

* [The number of vibrations of a C tuning-fork is 512. The deepest tone of orchestral instruments is the E of the double bass, with 41¼ vibrations. Some organs go as low as C′ with 33 vibrations, and some pianos may reach A with 27½ vibrations. In height the piano-forte reaches to a^{iv} with 3·520. The highest note of orchestra is probably d^v of the piccolo flute with 4·752 vibrations.]

SPECTRUM ANALYSIS EXPLAINED.

lowest upwards, the distinct notes of the complete octave would be heard.

What is it that here produces the sound? The mere revolution of the disk makes no noise; the motion of the air by the blowing through the tube first elicits the notes. When, by the rotation of the disk, the current of air strikes against an opening, it presses through it, pushing the air before it and condensing it; this impulse reaches the ear at once, and strikes upon the tympanum: the current of air immediately afterwards comes against the solid part between the holes, by which it is interrupted. If the circle blown upon contain twenty-four openings, the ear would receive twenty-four impulses at every revolution of the disk; and if the disk made twenty revolutions in a second, the ear would receive $20 \times 24 = 480$ impulses in the same interval. The outside circle has twice as many openings as the innermost one; it therefore furnishes with the same speed of rotation $20 \times 48 = 960$ impulses in a second.

The ear cannot distinguish individual impulses when they exceed sixteen in a second; the impressions they then produce become blended together, the one following the other so instantly that the sensation in the ear is that of one continuous impulse or sound.

The *pitch* of a note is thus seen to depend entirely upon the number of successive impulses following each other at the same uniform rate, its *strength* upon the force of the impulse. With a stronger blast, the pitch of the note remains unchanged, but the tone becomes more piercing, while if a ring containing a greater number of holes be blown upon, the pitch rises till in the last circle, with double the number of openings, the octave of the same note is heard that was given by the innermost circle.

It is true that the cause of sound is not the same in all musical instruments; sometimes it is the vibration of strings, or elastic prongs, sometimes stretched membranes, or, again, columns of air confined in tubes which create at regular periods a condensation and rarefaction of the air; but in every case a note can only be produced by similar impulses recurring at regular intervals, conveyed by the air to the organs of hearing.

Savart exhibited the cause of sound in another way which is not less instructive than the one just described. Instead of the perforated disk, he made use of a wheel provided with six hundred teeth, which could be set in very rapid rotation in the same manner as the disk, and as the wheel revolved, the teeth were allowed to press against the edge of a card. To make this experiment, it is only necessary to substitute a toothed or cog wheel for the perforated disk, and while the wheel is in rapid revolution, to hold a thin card, or a piece of pasteboard against its toothed edge. The card is bent a little by each tooth as it goes by, and springs back to its first position as soon as it is released by the passing of the tooth: the motion of the card is communicated to the surrounding air, and reaches the ear in consequence of the regular revolution of the wheel, in the form of waves of air, or of condensations and rarefactions of the air following each other at regular intervals.

When the wheel is turned slowly, there is heard only a succession of taps, or isolated impulses of the card, distinctly separable one from another, which do not as yet unite to form a musical sound. In proportion, however, as the rapidity of the rotation is increased, the number of impulses increases also, and they unite in the ear to produce musical notes rising continually in pitch. A small recording apparatus, fixed to the axle of the toothed wheel, gives the number of revolutions in a second; if this number be multiplied by six hundred, the number of teeth on the wheel, the result gives the number of condensations of air striking the ear in a second. It is easy by this means to determine the number of vibrations the ear receives in a second from a note of any given pitch, and thus to verify the results obtained by the perforated disk.

It will now be easier to understand the motion of ether, and its mode of operation on the organs of sight. Ether, as well as air, can be set in regular vibrations, and even in such a manner that the phases of condensation and rarefaction are repeated at regular periods of time. The difference between the vibrations of the air and the ether is occasioned by the remarkable delicacy and elasticity of the latter, which not only permits a greater rapidity in the propagation of motion than is possible with the coarse and heavy particles of air, but also allows the number of vibrations per second to be immensely greater, so that their number has to be reckoned by billions.

Analogy between Musical Sounds and Colors.

Colors are to the eye what musical tones are to the ear. A certain number of ether impulses in a second against the retina of the eye are necessary to produce the sensation of light: if the number of these waves pass above or below a certain limit, the eye is no longer sensible of them as *light*.

The first sensation of these vibrations on the part of the eye commences at about four hundred and fifty billion impulses in a second, and the eye ceases to perceive them when they have reached double this number, or about eight hundred billion: in the first case, the impression produced is that of dark red; in the latter, of deep violet.

The greater the number of vibrations in any given time, the more rapidly must the single impulses succeed each other; it may be concluded, therefore, that the different colors are only produced by the different degrees of rapidity with which the ether vibrations recur, just as the various notes in music depend upon the rapidity of the succession of vibrations of air. The vibrations which recur most slowly, — amounting, however, to at least four hundred and fifty billion in a second, — give the sensation of red; those recurring more rapidly produce that of yellow; and if the rapidity with which the impulses succeed each other continue to increase, the sensation becomes in succession green, blue, and violet, with which last color the human eye becomes insensible to the ether motion, which, however, is still very far from having attained its limit of rapidity.

The gradation of the colors from red through yellow, green, and blue, to violet, is to the eye what the gamut is to the ear; and it is therefore not without reason that we speak of the tone and harmony of color. To the physicist the words color and tone are only different modes of expression for similar and closely allied phenomena; they express the perception of regular movements recurring in equal periods of time, — in ether, producing colors; in air, musical sounds; in the former instance, by means of the organs of sight; in the latter, by the organs of hearing, — movements of extreme rapidity in ether, of more moderate speed in air.

But it will be asked what becomes of those vibrations which are above and below the limits of the eye's sensibility to light and color? Do they wander about purposeless and unnoticed? By no means: forces are proved to exist in the rays of the sun, and other intensely luminous bodies, which cannot be perceived by the eye. Those slower vibrations which, though they are reckoned by billions in a second, do not yet amount to four hundred and fifty billion, are made apparent to us in the sensation of heat, which is also the result of oscillatory movement — radiant heat being, like light, propagated without the aid of foreign bodies. Those vibrations, on the other hand, which have a velocity greater than that by which deep violet is produced — at which color the eye's susceptibility to light ceases — reveal themselves by their powerful chemical action; they succeed each other too rapidly for the visual nerves to be any longer conscious of the impulses, but they have the power of working chemical changes, and the decomposition of various substances can be undoubtedly traced to the agency of these invisible rays. An English physicist has succeeded in moderating the excessive velocity of these vibrations by means of certain substances, and in this way has brought some of the invisible chemical rays within reach of the eye's susceptibility.*

Dove describes, in his own ingenious manner, the course of the vibrations as they produce successively sound, heat, and light, as follows: —

"In the middle of a large, darkened room let us suppose a rod, set in vibration and connected with a contrivance for continually augmenting the speed of its vibrations. I enter the room at the moment when the rod is vibrating four times in a second. Neither eye nor ear tell me of the presence of the rod, only the hand, which feels the strokes when brought within their reach. The vibrations become more rapid, till when they reach the number of thirty-two in a second,† a deep hum strikes my ear. The tone rises continually in pitch, and passes through all the intervening grades up to the highest, the shrillest note; then all sinks again into the former grave-like silence. While full of astonishment at what I have heard, I feel suddenly (by the increased velocity of the vibrating rod) an agreeable warmth, as from a fire, diffusing itself from the spot whence the sound had pro-

---

* [Fluorescent substances possess this property. The peculiar blue light diffused from a perfectly colorless solution of sulphate of quinine was observed by Sir John Herschel, and the colored light diffused from various vegetable solutions and essential oils was subsequently examined by Sir David Brewster. To Professor Stokes, however, is due the true explanation of these phenomena; he showed that the blue light of the solution of quinine consists of vibrations brought within the limits of the power of the eye which were originally too rapid to be visible. If a fresh infusion of the bark of the horse-chestnut be placed beyond the limits of the visible spectrum of sunlight admitted through a slit into a dark room, it becomes beautifully luminous, in consequence of the power which it possesses to lower the invisible ultra-violet vibrations into light which can affect the eye.]

† That is to say, the tympanum is pressed in sixteen times, and sixteen times withdrawn; therefore sixteen blows are received upon the ear.

ceeded. Still all is dark. The vibrations increase in rapidity, and a faint red light begins to glimmer; it gradually brightens till the rod assumes a vivid red glow, then it turns to yellow, and changes through the whole range of colors up to violet, when all again is swallowed up in night. Thus nature speaks to the different senses in succession; at first, a gentle word, audible only in immediate proximity, then a louder call from an ever-increasing distance, till finally her voice is borne on the wings of light from regions of immeasurable space."

The Colors of Natural Objects.

Besides the colors of the spectrum, which are the simple elements composing white light, there is another class of colors apparent in every substance, which are therefore known as the colors of natural objects. When we see that a picture is formed by covering the canvas with various pigments, and that leaves and flowers are bright with the most beautiful tints, while white cloth becomes red, green, or blue, according to the color of the liquid into which it is dipped, we are easily led to believe that every substance carries in itself its own color, which is peculiar to it alone, and is inherent in the substance. At most, we might admit that light was requisite to render the color visible.

And yet this is not so. Were colors really something inherent in the object, every colored substance would manifestly appear always of the same color, by whatever light it was illuminated. But this, as every one knows, is not the case. The beautiful violet dress, which in daylight appears of the purest color, seems dull and gloomy by gaslight; materials which in daylight are a bright blue, are tinged with green in candle or lamp light. And what if the landscape, or a colored object, be viewed through a tinted glass? All colors then seem changed, without the objects in themselves being altered; if the color of the glass be intense, the various colors of the objects immediately disappear, and everything seems shaded in the color of the glass. The same thing happens if some common salt be rubbed into the wick of a spirit lamp, and surrounding objects viewed by the yellow light of such a flame; the colors disappear, or lose much of their brilliancy, and everything seems either in mere light and shade, or else of a dull gray.

These facts clearly prove that colors are not inherent in objects, that they have no independent existence, but that they are called forth by some extraneous cause.

On the other hand, these considerations show that there must be something in the objects themselves to help in the formation of color; for they in no way assume the color of the light illuminating them, but appear, as a rule, of quite a different hue.

The *natural* color of an object is that in which it appears when illuminated by the pure white light of the sun, or by daylight; it is called red or blue when it so appears by daylight. Now if an object be illuminated by white light, and yet appear of another color, the cause of the change must be looked for in the influence which the surface of the body exercises on the ether waves constituting white light. The effects of this influence are very different, according to the nature of the coloring matter with which the object is provided; but they may mostly be reduced to one of two cases — either that a portion of the ether motion is entirely stopped, or so considerably diminished in its passage over the ponderable atoms of the substance, as that heat, instead of light, is evolved, — or else that the ether waves are irregularly reflected from the surface of the object, as sometimes occurs with the waves of sound. In the first case, the rays of light are said to be *absorbed;* in the latter, *scattered.*

When the surface of a body has the property of absorbing all the colors of the solar spectrum with the exception of one, — the red, for example, — that body appears red to us by daylight, because this color alone is reflected to the eye.

When, on the contrary, it has the power of absorbing some of the rays,—the red and orange, for instance,—and of reflecting the others, namely, the yellow, green, and blue, the color of the object will then be that produced by the mixture of the unabsorbed — the reflected — colors. Now as white light contains the whole range of colors visible in the spectrum, it can easily be understood why so many different colored objects should be seen in nature with such an infinite variety of tints.*

When all the colors of white light are reflected from an object in the same proportions as they occur in the solar spectrum, the object appears white by daylight, and brilliant in proportion to the *quantity* of light it reflects. In proportion, however, as it reflects *fewer* rays of all kinds, the white loses in intensity; the object appears first gray, then dark, and at last black, when all the rays falling upon it are absorbed, and none reflected.

Those objects are therefore black the surfaces of which are so constituted as to absorb all the colored rays of white light; those are white which reflect all the rays which fall upon the surface; and those are colored which reflect some of the rays and absorb others.

A white object may therefore appear of all colors: if red light falls upon it, it reflects it to the eye, and appears red; in blue light, it appears blue; in green light, green, etc.; whereas a black object always appears black, whatever may be the color of the light by which it is illuminated.

We may here further remark that a colored substance assumes a different tint when illuminated by colored light, and then appears of another than its natural, that is to say, daylight color. Vermilion, for example, when placed in red light, becomes of a more fiery red; in orange or yellow

* [A certain proportion of the light falling upon colored bodies is usually sent back unchanged by superficial reflection, without undergoing the elective absorption to which the color of the substance is due.]

light, it appears orange or yellow, but deeper in tone; green rays impart to it something of their own tint, but as the red substance can reflect only a few of the green rays, it appears pale and dull by their light; it seems still duller and darker in blue light, and with indigo and violet it is almost black.

These phenomena are explained by the supposition that the surfaces of colored bodies possess the property of reflecting the rays of one particular color in far greater proportion than those of the other colors; they do not therefore appear black when illuminated by a light differing from their own natural color. Take, for example, a piece of paper half of which is colored a deep blue and half red: the colored rays other than the blue and red are not all absorbed: it is true that the blue piece reflects the blue rays pre-eminently and in greatest number, as the red part does the red rays, but the red has also the capability of reflecting other rays to a small amount. If the pure yellow light of a spirit flame impregnated with salt be allowed to fall on the paper in a completely dark room, the paper must appear black if the coloring matter reflect only the red and blue rays, because the yellow rays of the burning sodium will be absorbed, and no other light falls upon the paper; but this is not the case. The paper only appears black on the blue part; the red half is still visibly colored, though of a decidedly yellow shade. We therefore conclude that the blue of the paper does not reflect the yellow rays, but that the red has that power in a small degree. Almost all colored objects act like the red paper; they reflect pre-eminently one particular color, namely, that one of which they appear by daylight; but they are able also to reflect in small quantities all other, or at least some other colors, and so they vary in tint according to the kind of light in which they are seen.

The colors of objects are very rarely pure and simple, like those of the spectrum; most of them are composed of several colors, and can be decomposed into their original elements by a prism. As without prismatic decomposition, we are unable merely from the color of an object to say positively which colors are absorbed and which reflected, so it is equally impossible for us to decide, from the color of a flame, what the composition of its light may be, without investigation. The light of the sun, the lime-light, the magnesium light, the light of coal gas, petroleum, and oil, all appear to us more or less white, and yet the spectra of the various lights differ considerably. It is true they all contain the whole range of the colors of the spectrum, from red to violet; but each color is present in very different proportions. The light from gas, oil, and candles has less blue than that of the sun and the lime-light, and very much less violet. A blue material will therefore reflect less blue by lamp, gas, or candle light than by daylight; the color will not only be flat and dull, but will have a touch of green in it, on account of the preponderance of yellow light. Blue and violet especially receive a green tinge by candle light, in which these colors appear much duller than in daylight; and indeed sometimes, according to the nature of the coloring matter employed, this tint is so decided that in artificial light many kinds of green cannot be distinguished from blue.

Absorption of Light by Solid Bodies.

By the term *absorption* we have already designated that action by which light, in its passage through certain media, or by its reflection from the surfaces of bodies, is weakened, partially retained, or entirely stopped. We found that those substances called black absorbed rays of every color, and reflected no light from their surfaces, and that most substances absorbed with great avidity rays of certain colors, while they were insensitive to others. The cause of this absorption is probably due to the vibrations of the ether being communicated to the ponderable molecular particles of the substance.

Similar phenomena are noticed when light is transmitted through colored glass. When all the objects in a landscape appear red through a red glass, it is because the glass allows only the red rays to pass through, and absorbs every other colored ray: such a glass is transparent only to red light, and is opaque to every other color. But it is rarely the case that colored glass is transparent for one color only; most kinds of glass absorb rays of certain colors, and allow the others to pass through in very different proportions. The naked eye is unable to decide which of the colored rays are transmitted through a colored glass; this can only be accurately determined by analyzing the transmitted light by a spectroscope or simple prism.

If we examine by a spectroscope the transmitted light of the colored glass that we before made use of for obtaining red, green, and blue light, it will at once be seen that the ruby red glass transmits some orange and even some yellow rays, as well as the red, but that it entirely absorbs the green, blue, and violet rays; the cobalt blue glass transmits some violet and green rays, besides the blue, but absorbs all the red rays. If both glasses be laid one over the other, and a gas flame looked at through them, it seems as if scarcely a single ray was transmitted; the red glass absorbing the green, blue, and violet rays, and the blue glass absorbing the red rays, there pass through only traces of such light as has not been entirely absorbed, and this causes the gas flame to appear of a dull yellow. A combination of several glasses, or indeed any single glass which absorbs all the colored rays composing white light, is opaque, that is to say, black; glass of perfect transparency, absorbing absolutely none of the transmitted light, does not exist.

Relation between the Emission and the Absorption of Light.

When it is remembered that solid bodies in a state of incandescence *emit* a much greater body of light than gases emit in a similar condition, and that they are able to *absorb* a much greater quantity of the light falling on them, — in certain circumstances, even the whole of it, — through the transfer of the ether vibrations to their ponderable atoms; when, further, it is remembered that just those substances that *give out heat* with the greatest facility, and in the fullest quantity, are also the most capable of *receiving heat* from without, or *absorbing* it, the thought is suggested that there must be an intimate connection, a certain reciprocity between the power of a body to emit light (emission) and to absorb it (absorption). That the temperature of the substance has an influence on this relation between its emissive and absorptive powers, is proved by the phenomena of the gas spectra of the first, second, and third order, as well as by the variety of absorption spectra exhibited at different temperatures by the same substance. A century ago, the eminent mathematician and physicist, Euler, in his "Theoria lucis et caloris," enunciated the principle that every substance absorbs light of such a wave-length as coincides with the vibrations of its smallest particles. Foucault mentioned in his work on the spectrum of the electric light, published in 1849, that owing to the impurity of the carbon points, the intense yellow sodium line appeared, and was changed into a black line when sunlight was transmitted though the electric arc. Ångström gave expression, as early as the year 1853, to the general law that a gas, when luminous, *emits rays of light of the same refrangibility as those which it has power to absorb*, or, in other words, that *the rays which a substance absorbs are precisely those which it emits when made self-luminous.*

But all these facts remained isolated, and there was yet wanting the comprehensive grasp of a general physical law, under which the individual phenomena could be arranged. It was reserved to Kirchhoff to discover this law, and to establish triumphantly its truth, not only by mathematical proof, but also, in many striking instances, by experiment.

In the year 1860, he published his memoir on the relation between the emissive and absorptive powers of bodies for heat, as well as for light, in which occurs the celebrated sentence: "*The relation between the power of emission and the power of absorption of one and the same class of rays, is the same for all bodies at the same temperature,*" which will ever be distinguished as announcing one of the most important laws of nature, and which, on account of its extensive influence and universal application, will render immortal the name of its illustrious discoverer.

Reversal of the Spectra of Gases.

From Kirchhoff's law it follows as a necessary consequence that gases and vapors, in transmitting light, absorb or impair precisely those rays (colors) which they themselves emit, when rendered luminous, while they remain perfectly transparent to all other colored rays. Luminous sodium vapor, for example, gives, under ordinary circumstances, a spectrum of one bright yellow double line; it emits therefore this yellow light only. If the white light of the sun, the electric arc, or the oxyhydrogen lamp be allowed to pass through the vapor of sodium, the vapor will abstract or extinguish from the white light just those yellow rays which it emitted when in a luminous state. While the greater part of these yellow rays are absorbed by the sodium vapor, all the other rays — the red, orange, green, blue, and violet — pass through unimpaired.

The important result of these investigations is, therefore, that the characteristic *bright* lines of sodium, lithium, etc., are changed into *dark* lines when the intense white light of incandescent solid or liquid bodies passes through the vapor of these metals. The spectrum of luminous sodium vapor is a bright *yellow* (double) line, the rest of the field in the spectroscope remaining dark;[*] the spectrum of an incandescent solid or liquid body, after it has passed through sodium vapor at a lower temperature than itself, occupies on the contrary the whole field with its brilliant colors, excepting only that one place in which the *dark* sodium line is found. As therefore the bright lines of gas spectra are converted, in these experiments, into dark lines, while the dark parts of the spectrum are changed into brilliant colors by the continuous spectrum of the white light, the entire gas spectrum seems to be reversed in respect of its illumination: for this reason, the phenomenon has been called, after Kirchhoff, "*the reversal of the spectrum.*"

We can now readily predict what appearance will be presented in the spectroscope, if the light of an incandescent solid or liquid body, before entering the slit of the instrument, pass through a less highly heated atmosphere of any kind of vapor, such as that of sodium, lithium, iron, etc. The incandescent body would have produced a continuous spectrum, if its light had sustained no change on the way; but in the vaporous atmosphere through which its rays must pass, each vapor absorbs just those rays which it would have emitted if luminous, thereby extinguishing these particular colors, and substituting for them dark bands in those places of the continuous spectrum where it would have produced bright lines. The spectroscope shows therefore a continuous spectrum, extending through the whole range of colors, from red to violet, but intersected by dark lines; the sodium line, the two lithium lines, the numerous iron lines, etc., appear on the colored ground of the continuous spectrum as so many *dark* lines.

[*] See No. 3 of Frontispiece.

Spectra of this kind are evidently *absorption spectra;* they are also called *reversed* or *compound spectra.* If a *complete coincidence* can be established in such a spectrum, by means of either a prism of comparison, or a scale, between the characteristic *bright* lines of the gas spectrum of a certain substance, with the same number of *dark* lines, the conclusion may be admitted that in the absorptive atmosphere which has produced the dark lines, the same substance is contained in a condition of vapor.

The Solar Spectrum and the Fraunhofer Lines.

The most brilliant example of a reversed spectrum, — that is to say, a continuous spectrum, crossed by dark absorption lines, — is afforded by the sun. If an ordinary spectroscope, armed with a telescope of low power, be directed to a bright sky, with a rather wide opening of the slit, a magnificent continuous spectrum will be seen, exhibiting the most beautiful and brilliant colors, without either bright or dark lines. But if the slit be narrowed so as to obtain the purest possible spectrum, and the focus of the telescope be very accurately adjusted, the spectrum, now much fainter, will be seen to be crossed by a number of dark lines and cloudy bands. If, by the use of several prisms, the spectrum be lengthened, and a higher magnifying power employed, these thick lines and bands will become resolved into separate fine lines and groups of lines, which are so sharply defined and so characteristically grouped that, by the help of a scale, they are easily impressed upon the memory, and distinguished one from another.

As early as 1802, these dark lines in the solar spectrum had been observed and described by Wollaston; later, in 1814, they were more carefully examined and mapped by Fraunhofer, of Munich; and later still by Becquerel, Zantedeschi, Matthiessen, Brewster, Gladstone, and others; but their origin and nature remained a mystery, notwithstanding the acutest reasoning and most painstaking researches of many able physicists, until Kirchhoff made his splendid discovery in 1859.

Fraunhofer was able to distinguish with certainty about six hundred lines; he found also that with the same prism and telescope they always kept the same relative order and position, and were therefore peculiarly adapted to serve as marks for denoting the place of any single set of colored rays, and for determining the refrangibility of any particular color

To facilitate reference to any of the innumerable colors of the solar spectrum (Frontispiece, No. 1), Fraunhofer, whose drawing is accurately represented in Fig. IV., selected out of the great number he observed *eight* characteristic lines, situated in the most important places of the spectrum, which he designated by the letters A, B, C, D, E, F, G, H; of these lines A and B lie in the red, C in the red near the orange, D in the orange, forming a double line with a high power, E in the yellow, F on the borders of the green and blue, G in the dark blue or indigo, and H in the violet. Besides these lines, there is a noticeable group a, of fine lines between A and B, and also a group b, consisting of three fine lines, between E and F. It was remarked even by Fraunhofer that the position of the two dark lines in the solar spectrum designated by him D, were coincident with the two bright lines shown by the light of a lamp, now known as the double sodium line. These dark lines of the solar spectrum have been called, after their discoverer, the Fraunhofer lines.

Since Fraunhofer counted in the spectrum more than six hundred dark lines, Brewster has counted two thousand, and others, by causing the refracted rays to pass successively through several prisms (some using as many as nine at one observation), the existence of three thousand lines has been ascertained. These lines have been carefully mapped by Ångström and Thalén, and Kirchhoff, who has carefully

SPECTRUM ANALYSIS EXPLAINED.

studied them, and ascertained wherein they *coincide* with the bright lines of metals known to us, says, " The most striking coincidences between the spectrum lines of terrestrial elements and the dark lines of the solar spectrum are shown in iron, sodium, potassium, calcium, magnesium, manganese, chromium, nickel, and hydrogen; the spectrum lines of these substances not only agree exactly with the dark lines in *position* and *breadth*, but proclaim their relationship to them by a similar degree of intensity. The brighter, for instance, a spectrum line appears, so much the darker will its corresponding line be in the solar spectrum.

Fig. IV. shows the principal Fraunhofer lines, A, B, C, etc., and many intermediate ones. It also shows the coincidence between sixty-five of the bright lines in the spectrum of iron and the same number of dark lines in the solar spectrum, *proving beyond a doubt the existence of iron in the sun*. Other observations prove as conclusively the existence of sodium, potassium, and the other metals which are above mentioned.

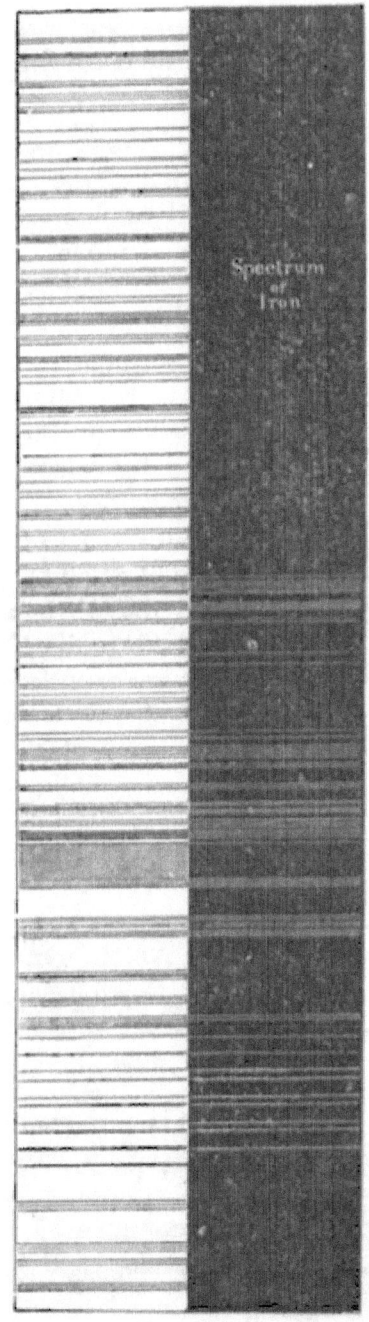

Fig. IV.

The Telluric Lines.

In addition to the Fraunhofer lines, there are other dark lines in the solar spectrum, which are called *atmospheric* or *telluric* lines. These are variable, and are caused by the varying condition of the earth's atmosphere. Janssen found them to be darkest at sunrise and sunset, and less intense in the middle of the day, a periodicity of change which at once proves their atmospheric origin, but they were never entirely absent from the spectrum. He instituted a series of experiments by which he found that a large number of the variable lines in the solar spectrum are due to the presence of *aqueous vapor* in the earth's atmosphere, and also a method secured for detecting the presence of aqueous vapor in the heavenly bodies.

Angström says that nearly all the changes of color observed in the red glow of sunrise and sunset find a simple explanation in the phenomena of atmospheric absorption, whereby all the ingenious and elaborate explanations hitherto attempted are completely set aside.

It is fully admitted that other heavenly bodies besides the earth may be surrounded by an atmosphere; Janssen's discovery of the spectrum of aqueous vapor furnishes the means of ascertaining whether this vapor, indispensable to the maintenance of all the living organisms of our planet, is also present in the other celestial bodies. Repeated observations undertaken by Janssen on the high mountains of Italy and Greece have already furnished proof that aqueous vapor is present in the atmospheres of the planets Mars and Saturn.

Spectrum Apparatus.

The thought is perhaps rising in the minds of many who have accompanied us thus far, that the production of the spectrum of a substance for the purposes of analytical examination is encumbered with great difficulties and many troublesome details, involving too much labor to be available for the use of the chemist and the physicist. This is, however, not the case; if, in our mode of illustration, a powerful galvanic battery, and the electric lamp, with its revolving table and large screen, have been employed, it has been only to show how, by the extraordinary heat and light of the voltaic arc, the simple phenomena on which spectrum analysis is based can be made visible to many hundred spectators at once in a large lecture-room. When, however, the light from the heated vapors need not be greater than is required for a single observer, the whole electric apparatus may be dispensed with, and the simple Bunsen burner substituted; in place of the large screen of paper that reflected the light, the small, sensitive screen of nerves — the retina of the human eye — becomes the surface on which the spectrum is received; and the whole cumbrous contrivance occupying so much space is replaced by a small spectrum apparatus as trustworthy as it is easy to manipulate.

FIG. V.

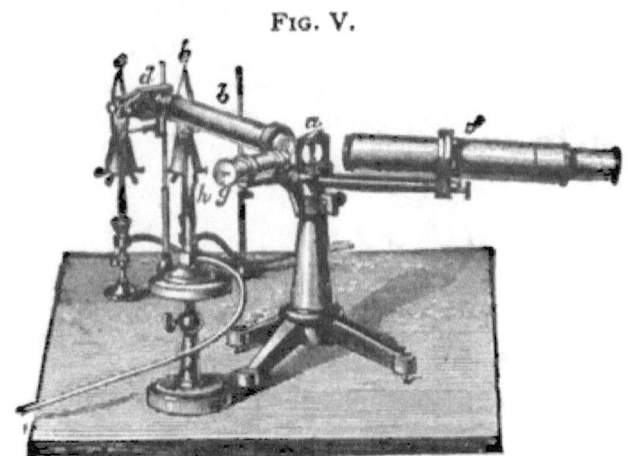

THE COMPOUND SPECTROSCOPE.

Fig. V. shows a compound spectroscope. With this we are enabled to use two flames, and the apparatus is so arranged that we can see the two spectra, one above the other, and compare them with each other. For instance, putting a small quantity of the substance we know to contain sodium into one flame, we place a substance supposed to contain sodium in the other flame, and then, by means of a small reflecting prism placed at the end of the slit, we have the spectra of both sent into the telescope, one above the other, and can tell at once whether the lines coincide with each other. Another arrangement for facilitating the comparison of spectra consists of the illuminated millimetre scale contained in the tube g (Fig. V.), a magnified reflection of which is thrown into the telescope f, from the surface of the prism a. The scale is thus seen *between* the two spectra, and the position of any line can be accurately measured, and ascertained.

The reader is now in a position to understand the use of the various parts of a complete spectrum apparatus, especially the three tubes directed to the prism at different angles, as in that constructed by Kirchhoff and Bunsen. The eye of the observer is placed in the axis of the telescope directed to that surface from which the light emerges in the form of a spectrum; the opposite surface of the prism receives through the slit and collimating lens the light emitted from the object to be examined; at the side of the observer is the tube carrying the illuminated scale, or the micrometer screw, so that the mark coinciding with any division of the scale may be placed on any line of the spectrum.

Conclusion.

If we have given our readers anything approaching an adequate idea of the beauty and utility of this wonderful discovery, we feel sure it will only stimulate them to investigate and study it further. It was our intention to have continued the subject, and closed this article with a *résumé* of the discoveries made by means of spectrum analysis, but we find it impossible to condense the matter sufficiently to bring it into a size appropriate to these papers, and we defer it to the next number, which will be devoted to *Spectrum Analysis Discoveries.*

5. Spectrum Analysis Discoveries,

Showing its Application in Microscopical Research, and to Discoveries of the Physical Constitution and Movements of

THE HEAVENLY BODIES.

IN the preceding article we gave our readers, in general terms, the scope of this great discovery, and its importance to the scientific world, and, to make it plainer, laid down in a condensed form the received laws of the theory of sound, heat, light, and color, as well as an explanation of the modes in use of detecting minute particles of elements, where all other means had failed. We also showed that, by means of it, many substances, before unknown, had been discovered; and it is not doubted that others will be in the future, as the discovery is still in its infancy.

THE MICROSPECTROSCOPE.

In addition to ordinary spectroscopes, Messrs. Sorby and Browning have devised a combination of the microscope and spectroscope, called the *microspectroscope*, which renders it possible to examine very minute traces of substances. This application of the spectroscope has been very useful in investigating substances which have special importance in physiology and pathology: thus in examining normal and diseased blood, in detecting albumen in urine, and in ascertaining the rate at which certain substances pass into the various fluids of the system, as well as investigating supposed cases of poisoning. The characteristic *absorption bands* which certain liquids, such as wine, beer, etc., present in their normal state, compared with those yielded by adulterated substances, furnish a delicate and certain means of detecting the latter.

An instance of its use in detecting the cause of impurity in water is related, as follows: The water used by the inhabitants of a crowded court, amongst whom several cases of typhoid fever had appeared, was drawn from a rather shallow well, and was highly charged with various unoxidized compounds of nitrogen. It was suspected that, from some defect of drainage, the contents of a public urinal obtained entrance to the well. The fact that the well-water contained seven times as much common salt as the normal water of the vicinity, was some confirmation of the suspicion. Professor Church obtained *absolute proof* of the fact by the following method. He introduced two grammes of a lithium salt into the urinal, and two hours later was enabled readily to detect with the spectroscope the presence of lithium in a litre of the well-water, which by previous examination had shown no traces of this substance. Many other instances of its use for similar purposes might be cited.

Spectrum analysis has thus opened a wide field of investigation to the physiologist, the physician, the botanist, the zoölogist, the chemist, and the technologist, and the labors undertaken in these various departments of science have already yielded valuable results.

It was shown in our last paper that by it we have at last the means of forming a definite idea of the physical constitution of the heavenly bodies, and ascertaining the existence of atmospheres around other planets, and other means of supporting life such as exist on this earth. We will proceed to give a *résumé* of the other discoveries regarding the physical constitution and movements of the heavenly bodies.

Kirchhoff's Theory of the Physical Constitution of the Sun.

It had long been assumed that the gaps in the colors of the solar spectrum which form the Fraunhofer dark lines, were due to an absorption of the corresponding colored rays in the atmosphere of the sun; but no explanation could be given of this phenomenon. The cause of this absorption was ascertained by Kirchhoff in his discovery that a vapor absorbs from white light just those rays which it emits when luminous, and he proved the whole system of the Fraunhofer lines to be mainly produced by the overlying of the reversed spectra of such substances as are to be found in the earth. He thus arrived at a new conception of the physical constitution of the sun which is entirely opposed to the theories held by Wilson and Sir William Herschel in explanation of the solar spots.

According to Kirchhoff, the sun consists of a *solid* or *partially liquid* nucleus in the highest state of incandescence, which emits, like all incandescent solid or liquid bodies, every possible kind of light, and therefore would of itself give a *continuous* spectrum without any dark lines. This incandescent central nucleus is surrounded by an *atmosphere* of lower temperature, containing, on account of the extreme heat of the nucleus, the vapors of many of the substances of which this body is composed. The rays of light, therefore, emitted by the nucleus, must pass through this atmosphere before reaching the earth, and each vapor extinguishes from the white light those rays which it would itself emit in a glowing state. Now it is found, when the sun's light is analyzed by a prism, that a multitude of rays are extinguished, and just those rays which would be emitted by the vapors of sodium, iron, calcium, magnesium, etc., were they made self-luminous; consequently the vapors of the following substances, sodium, iron, potassium, calcium, barium, magnesium, manganese, titanium, chromium, nickel, cobalt, hydrogen, and probably, also, zinc, copper, and gold, must exist in the solar atmosphere, and these metals, therefore, must also be present to a considerable extent in the body of the sun.

Could the light from the sun's nucleus in any way be set aside, and only that of the incandescent vapors of the sun's atmosphere be received through the slit of the spectroscope, a spectrum would then be obtained composed of the actual spectra of these substances, that is to say, the same system of bright colored lines which now appear as the dark Fraunhofer lines.

The Solar Spots; The Faculæ and their Spectra.

It would lead us too far from our subject were we to dwell upon the phenomena of the solar spots, important as they are for acquiring a knowledge of the physical constitution of the sun, or enter upon a full description of their form, their mode of formation and disappearance, their motion, their connection with the sun's rotation upon its axis, their periodic occurrence, and the various hypotheses that have been formed as to their nature; but, on the other hand, we must still less be silent on the subject, since spectrum analysis has investigated these wonderful appearances with a success which has added much to our knowledge of the constitution of the sun.

Fig. 6 shows a remarkable group of solar spots. These, and indeed a large proportion of solar spots, consist principally of a dark, almost black, central portion, the *umbra** surrounded by a space somewhat less dark called the *penumbra:* the umbra has generally an irregular form, while the penumbra exhibits a structure radiating towards the centre.

If the sun be observed with a high power, the surface presents by no means a uniform appearance; a multitude of bright and dark stripes cross each other in all directions, and

---

* The dark central part of a spot has been distinguished throughout by the name *umbra*, in accordance with the usual custom of astronomers. Mr. Dawes showed that within this part of a spot one or more darker spots may generally be observed, to which he gave the name of *nucleus*.

Fig. VI.

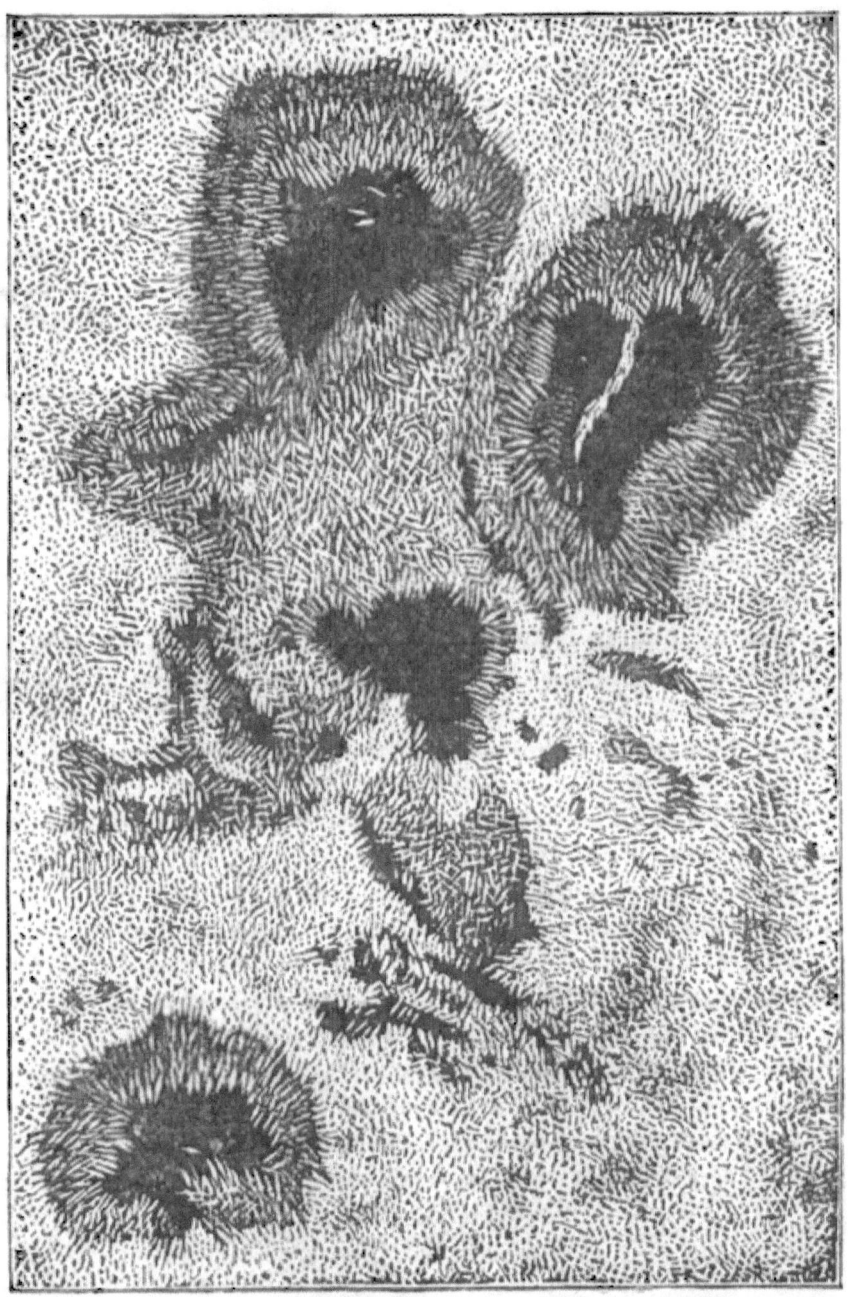

Group of Solar Spots observed and drawn by Nasmyth, 5th June, 1864.

the luminous surface appears like a net of bright meshes interwoven with dark threads and small dark pores. The brightest portions (Fig. 6) show a more or less elongated form, which suggested to Nasmyth the name of "willow leaves," while Dawes compares them to "bits of straw," and Huggins calls them merely "granules."

On this uneven and ever-varying bright background the spots make their appearance in the greatest variety of form and size. The penumbra not unfrequently stretches across the black central portion in various places (see right hand spot, Fig. 6), and generally appears much darker at the outer edges, where the spot touches the bright part of the sun's surface, than in other places. Very often the penumbra is traversed by few or more bright curved bands, stretching from the outer edge towards the nucleus, generally at right angles to the confines of the nucleus and penumbra, which give the spot the appearance as if a number of streams of some luminous matter had broken through the dam formed by the penumbra, to fall into the abyss of the umbra. (See central spot, Fig. 6.) Even the umbra itself is often crossed by one or more broad luminous bands called *bridges*, by which it is divided into several portions.

Besides the dark spots, and chiefly in their immediate neighborhood, bright places make their appearance on the sun's surface, which have been called *faculæ*. They are generally the attendants of solar spots, and are especially to be seen at the extreme edge of the penumbra when the spot has reached the sun's limb, that is, its edge or border; that they are not the effect of contrast between the dark spot and the neighboring brightness, is proved by the circumstance that every spot is not accompanied by faculæ, and that very frequently isolated faculæ are to be seen, which are almost always the precursor of a coming spot.

The faculæ, like the spots, vary considerably in form; generally they are round and concentrated, but often they have the appearance of long stripes of light, disposed like veins, converging from all sides towards a spot.

The wreathed faculæ are almost always followed in a few days by the appearance of a group of spots; among the vein-like waves of light visible in many places, more especially towards the sun's limb, there is first developed a dull scar-like place out of which the spots are formed, sometimes singly, and sometimes in groups; and not unfrequently the formation of a spot may be predicted from the increased intensity of light at that place on the sun's disk.

When a spot is observed near the sun's limb or edge in the midst of the surrounding faculæ, it is difficult to avoid the impression that the spot lies in a hollow between bright overhanging mountains; and it was observed by Secchi on the 5th of August, 1865, that the faculæ, when they reached the western limb of the sun, appeared like small projections and irregularities upon the sharply defined limb of the sun.

Although the real connection between the faculæ and the spots is not yet fully understood, it may be safely concluded from these observations that the spots lie deeper in the solar surface than do the faculæ, and that these faculæ are mountainous elevations of the luminous matter forming the photosphere, by which the spot is surrounded in a wide circuit as by a wall.

The group of solar spots observed and drawn by Nasmyth on the 5th of June, 1864, is given in Fig. 6, in which all the details characteristic of a spot are to be recognized — the black umbra, the penumbra in a variety of forms, composed of the "leaves" directed towards the umbra, and the surrounding luminous surface of the sun presenting its usual granulated appearance. This surface is called the *photosphere*, a name given without reference to any particular theory as to its physical constitution or structure. The photosphere is entirely covered with *pores*, or small spots, less luminous than the other parts; where they congregate, and become conspicuous by forming a black umbra and shaded penumbra, they constitute the ordinary *solar spot;* where the portions of greater brilliancy than the surrounding parts of the photosphere congregate, they form the *faculæ*, and these generally accompany the spots, or precede their formation.

If a solar spot be watched in the telescope from day to day, or from hour to hour, it will soon be seen to change in form; it increases or diminishes, or completely vanishes away, while new spots make their appearance. In the process of disappearing, the dark umbra first gradually contracts until it becomes invisible, leaving the dusky penumbra perceptible for some time longer. Not unfrequently a spot breaks up into several spots, and occasionally a group unites to form one, and sometimes, even, one spot is seen to pass over another, partially covering it, and then withdrawing from it. In all these changes, the spots exhibit an amount of mobility displayed in general only by liquid or vaporous masses.

The formation and changes in the configuration of a spot may often be watched during the course of observation, and it not unfrequently happens that the appearance of a group of spots is so entirely changed from one day to another, that it can no longer be recognized in the new form it has assumed.

On the other hand, there are spots presenting scarcely any change, which preserve nearly the same form for many days together. Spots of this kind are of the highest value to the astronomer, as they afford the only means of ascertaining the time of the revolution of the sun upon its axis, the position of this axis, and its inclination to the earth's orbit.

It not unfrequently happens, that the same spot which has been observed to disappear on the western limb has, in the course of about fourteen days, been seen to reappear on the eastern limb, and in the lapse of another fourteen days has disappeared a second time on the western limb — a phenomenon that proves beyond a doubt that the spots are connected with the surface of the sun, and that the sun itself has a revolution upon its axis. If the time required for the earth's motion round the sun be allowed for in this revolution of the spot, the result will show, according to Spörer, a mean time of rotation for the sun amounting to twenty-five days, five hours, thirty-eight minutes.

Kirchhoff considers these forms to be cloud-like condensations in the sun's atmosphere, which are produced by the loss of the solar heat by radiation, in the same way as the aqueous vapors of the earth's atmosphere are formed into mist and cloud. When such clouds arise over the bright and glowing surface of the sun, they obscure the light of the sun at that spot, and it is but natural that these cloudy masses, so irregularly formed, should also become further condensed, or be dispersed with the same amount of irregularity, according as they come in contact with cooler or warmer streams of gas.

The results of the spectrum observations of Secchi, Lockyer, and Young, important and valuable as they are, remain as yet too isolated and unconnected with telescopic observations of the spots and faculæ to yield material sufficient for explaining the nature of these forms. This much, however, may be regarded as certain — that the phenomena of the increase in the width and intensity of the Fraunhofer lines, as well as the appearance of new dark bands in the spectrum of the umbra, *are produced by the increased absorptive power exercised by the substances of which the spot is formed.*

When the white light of the sun's nucleus which has already suffered absorption from the absorptive stratum passes through the vaporous matter of a spot, it undergoes a yet further absorption from the additional matter which the spot contains. As, therefore, the lines of calcium and iron are considerably affected in the spectrum of a spot, the sodium lines in a smaller degree, and to some extent those of magnesium, it may be concluded that the substance forming the solar spots is composed pre-eminently of vapors of calcium, iron, titanium, sodium, barium, and magnesium, and that these substances occur in layers of varying thickness, and in very different proportions.

That hydrogen gas constitutes an important element in the formation of the spots, is shown in the most unequivocal manner by the spectrum. The hydrogen lines are most affected in the parts that lie close to the umbra, in the bridge, when one is formed, and in the penumbra.

An explanation of this phenomenon is, that hydrogen gas breaks forth, from time to time, from the interior of the incandescent solar nucleus. Owing to its extreme lightness, this gas would rise in enormous pillars of flame (prominences) over the absorptive vaporous stratum of the photosphere, and, in consequence of the cooling ensuing from expansion, would enter into a variety of chemical combinations, especially with oxygen; the uncombined part would then flow to the side, while that in combination with oxygen (steam) and the other solar substances would form gaseous or vaporous masses, which, from their nature as well as from their continued cooling, would be heavier than the hydrogen gas, and would sink down from their greater gravity. It is to be expected that the stream of gas on rising would carry up with it a quantity of those substances that exist in the sun's nucleus and the surounding stratum of absorptive vapor (the photosphere); if these substances, themselves incandescent, were present in sufficient quantities in the luminous hydrogen gas, their characteristic lines would be seen as bright lines in the spectrum of the pillars of flame. During the recent total eclipses, many such lines were in fact observed, together with the bright hydrogen lines, in the prominences, a description of which will be given farther on; they can now be observed daily, sometimes in great numbers, upon the sun's disk.

When the force of the gas eruption has somewhat subsided, and the chemical combinations ensue, producing vaporous precipitations of many kinds, the formation of the spot begins. The heavier portions of these precipitations sink down, and form the *umbra* of a spot at the place of greatest condensation, while the parts which are less dense constitute the *penumbra*. The vaporous umbra, however, though apparently quite black, is yet able to transmit a considerable amount of sunlight; indeed, according to Zöllner's measurements, the black umbra of a spot emits *four thousand times* as much light as that derived from an equal area of the full moon. This statement is fully confirmed by the results of spectrum analysis, for even the blackest umbra yields a spectrum exhibiting all the details of full sunlight.

The various remarkable changes which the lines of hydrogen, magnesium, sodium, calcium, and iron suffer in the spectrum of the umbra, seem to show that in the cloud-like and vaporous substances constituting the spot, the new combinations are disposed in layers, according to their specific gravity. Thus hydrogen gas occupies the highest stratum; aqueous vapor, magnesium, and sodium follow in thinner layers below; and the heavier vapors of calcium, titanium, and iron form the lowest and densest stratum, the base of the spot.

The formation of a spot will accordingly immediately follow an eruption of hydrogen; the spot itself is a dense, cloudy, luminous mass, probably of a semi-fluid consistency, composed of many constituents — according to Zöllner, a kind of scoria — which sinks by its gravity a certain depth into the photosphere, or outer portion of the sun, and partially intercepts the light from the lower stratum of the photosphere, therefore presenting to us the appearance of a dark mass projected upon the disk of the sun, in the same way as the exceedingly intense light of the oxyhydrogen lime-light appears black when seen against the sun.

The enormous dimensions of these dense masses of vapor, which extend sometimes in all directions, account for the length of time the spots continue visible, not unfrequently remaining during several rotations of the sun. Their disappearance is to be explained partly by the substance of the photosphere flowing into the cavity of the spot, partly by the complete subsidence of the vapors into the nucleus of the sun, where, in consequence of the enormous heat, the compound substances which may exist in them are broken up into their original elements.

These conjectures are by no means intended to afford a complete explanation of all the phenomena of a solar spot. Though it certainly is of the highest interest for us to acquire a knowledge of the physical nature of that heavenly body whence we derive light, heat, motion, and life, we must yet be cautious of receiving for truth what is only the result of speculation, especially as the theories on this subject rest on isolated observations which are too unconnected to point to any certain conclusion. The suggestions here thrown out are only intended, therefore, to throw some light upon the results hitherto obtained by the spectrum observations of Secchi, Huggins, Lockyer, and Young, and by affording an unconstrained interpretation of them to bring them into harmony with the phenomena observed during the total solar eclipses of 1868, 1869, and 1871.

Total Solar Eclipses.

The reason why our knowledge concerning the nature of the sun is still so imperfect, is that the remarkable phenomena occurring on the sun's limb are so completely overpowered by the blinding light of the solar nucleus or photosphere, that they remain invisible even in the most powerful telescopes. It is not sufficient to get rid of the sun's rays by the interposition of an opaque screen, because the diffused light of the sky cannot be eliminated by this means, and this light, even, is so intense as to conceal the faint light of the sun's appendages. It is quite otherwise, however, during a *total eclipse* of the sun; then the moon covers the whole of the sun's disk, and includes a large tract of the earth's surface in the cone of its shadow, revealing to the observer, who is no longer hindered by the light of day, a display of phenomena round the sun which can be seen in no other way, and the study of which is peculiarly fitted to throw light on the nature and physical constitution of the sun.

We will not suffer ourselves to be detained by a description of those changes that pass over the landscape as the darkness advances, nor dwell upon the deep impression which the sudden disappearance of the last rays of the sun, and the equally sudden reappearance of the light, make both upon men and animals.

The diameter of the cone of the shadow thrown by the moon towards the earth, amounts at the spot where it touches the earth's surface on the equator during the time of totality to about 122 miles: as, however, the moon, which throws the shadow, only completes its course in the heavens round the earth from west to east in one month, and the earth, which receives the shadow, accomplishes its revolution from west to east in one day, it follows that the motion of the moon's shadow is very much slower than that of the earth's surface. It therefore happens that the earth appears to run away from under the moon's shadow, or that the moon's shadow seems to run over the earth from east to west. From an elevated position the shadow of the moon is seen to approach with enormous rapidity, and the sensation as though a material substance, such as a terrific cloud of smoke, were rushing over the earth's surface, fills the uninitiated spectator with fear and dread. A few minutes before the commencement of the totality, the brightest stars become visible, and the sharply defined black edge of the moon appears surrounded on all sides by a very narrow but very brilliant ring of light, of silver whiteness, which is called the *corona*. From the corona faint rays of light, irregular in length and breadth, stream out in all directions, surrounding the moon's disk like a glory, whence this crown of rays is usually designated the glory or *halo*.

When the total darkness has commenced, the *prominences* make their appearance, which are cloud-like masses of a rose or pale coral color, disposed either singly or in groups, at various places on the moon's limb.

They pierce the corona in the most wonderful forms, sometimes as single outgrowths of enormous height, sometimes as low projections spreading far along the moon's limb. The prominences are generally first seen on the eastern (left) side of the sun, where at the commencement of the totality the moon only grazes the sun's edge, and the space immediately surrounding the sun is yet uncovered; in proportion as the moon advances to the east, the space immediately surrounding the western parts of the sun becomes free, and the prominences are then seen also on that side in greater number, and developed with much greater distinctness.

There remains now no longer any doubt that these remarkable phenomena belong to the sun, and are great accumulations of the luminous gaseous material by which the solar body is wholly surrounded; it cannot therefore greatly astonish us that their forms have been seen to change even during the short duration of the totality; that which calls much more for wonder is the enormous height to which these pillars of gas extend beyond the limb of the sun, a height which in some instances exceeds ninety thousand miles.

THE TOTAL SOLAR ECLIPSE OF THE 7TH OF AUGUST, 1869.

This eclipse was invisible in Europe; the zone of totality stretched from Alaska, where the eclipse began at noon, over British America and the south-west corner of Minnesota, then crossed the Mississippi near Burlington (Iowa), and passed through Illinois, Western Virginia, and North

Carolina, reaching the Atlantic Ocean in the neighborhood of Beaufort.

The event excited the most lively interest among astronomers and photographers throughout the whole of North America, and occasioned the equipment of a number of scientific expeditions, which were also supplemented by the valuable labors of many private individuals. The observers were in almost every instance favored with the finest weather, and their efforts were rewarded by a large collection of photographic pictures, and many valuable spectroscopic and other observations. That portion of the zone of totality which traversed the inhabited parts of the United States was studied everywhere with telescopes, spectroscopes, and other instruments of observation, so that the whole of this tract of country became one vast observatory. Although the duration of totality was less than in the eclipse observed in India (1868), yet the phenomenon was attended on the whole with many more favorable circumstances; the heat was less intense, the places suitable for observation were much more conveniently situated, and the sun's altitude was not so great as in the eclipse of 1868. The most important points of investigation had reference to the scrutiny of the prominences by means of photography and the spectroscope, the examination of the nature of the corona, and the search for planets between Mercury and the Sun.

The most complete expeditions were those sent out from Washington, one from the Nautical Almanac Office, the astronomical department being under the charge of Professor Coffin, while the photographic arrangements were conducted by Professor Henry Morton, of Philadelphia: another expedition was despatched from the United States Naval Observatory, under the superintendence of Commodore B. F. Sands.

The first expedition, under the guidance of Professor Morton, selected stations in the State of Iowa, as follows:—

1. Burlington, where the observers were Professor Mayer,

and Messrs. Kendall, Willard, Phillipps, and Mahoney, together with Dr. C. A. Young, Professor of Dartmouth College (Hanover), well known as an experienced spectroscopist, and Dr. B. A. Gould, to whose charge the photographic department was committed;

2. Ottumwa, where Professor Himes, and Messrs. Zentmayer, Moelling, Brown, and Baker, were stationed;

3. Mount Pleasant, occupied by Professor Morton, and Messrs. Wilson, Clifford, Cremer, Ranger, and Carbutt, as well as by some other Professors, including Pickering, who were desirous of making astronomical observations on the physical phenomena of the eclipse.

Stations selected by the second expedition: —

1. Des Moines (Iowa), where Professor Newcomb undertook the observation of the corona and the search for intermercurial planets, Professor Harkness the spectroscopic investigations, and Professor Eastman the meteorological department. Several other gentlemen skilled in solar photography associated themselves with these observers.

2. Bristol (Tennessee), where Bardwell, who undertook the observation of the corona, and other observers were stationed.

Besides these most important expeditions, furnished with the most admirable and complete means of observation, several scientific men were engaged at various points in the zone of totality, either in observing the astronomical details of the eclipse, or in investigating the prominences, the corona, and their spectra. Among these may be mentioned Dr. Edward Curtis, who at Des Moines obtained no fewer than one hundred and nineteen pictures of the different phases of the eclipse; W. S. Gilman, by whom some most valuable observations were instituted at St. Paul Junction (Iowa) upon the connection between the solar spots, the faculæ, and the prominences; J. A. Whipple, who with Professor Winlock and several assistants procured at Shelbyville (Kentucky) eighty photographic pictures, six of which were taken

SPECTRUM ANALYSIS DISCOVERIES.

during the totality, one of them exhibiting a complete and magnificent corona; as well as Professor G. W. Hough, Director of the Dudley Observatory, who in company with nine fellow-observers recorded all the details of the eclipse at Mattoon (Illinois).

Out of the mass of materials afforded by the observations of this eclipse, it will only come within our province to communicate those results which have reference to the physical constitution of the sun, and were obtained partly by photographic delineation, and partly by the help of the spectroscope. The course of the eclipse and the photographic work carried on at Mount Pleasant, where the totality lasted two minutes, forty-eight seconds, is described by Wilson nearly as follows: —

"For some days prior to the eclipse, the sky was overcast, and threatened rain; but the 7th of August was bright, without a cloud, such a day as had not occurred for months, and the sun shone with remarkable clearness and warmth. The moment of first contact arrived; the first plate was already placed in the tube; Professor Watson signalled to us the moment for exposure by a motion of the hand; the instantaneous shutter was opened and closed, and the first picture was taken. We thus commenced a series of pictures taken at intervals of five or ten minutes till the commencement of totality, after which the series was continued on the re-appearance of the sun till the termination of the eclipse. Darkness came on with the totality, but not the darkness of night; still it rendered reading impossible. The amount of light upon the landscape was scarcely equal to that of bright moonlight, yet it was sufficient for us to pursue our work. An instant before the commencement of totality, the thin crescent of the sun was still quite dazzling; then the light went out as from an expiring candle.

"There, between heaven and earth, hung face to face the two great luminaries, sun and moon, a large black round spot encircled by a brilliant ring of deep gold-colored light, interrupted here and there by the brighter spots of the flesh-colored prominences of irregular size and form, and surrounded by the magnificent corona, which shot out rays in every direction, faintest where the prominences were most conspicuous, but enveloping the whole with a glory which was marvellously beautiful, as if the Creator were about to show His omnipotence in this wonder. The phenomenon resembled a gigantic image from a magic lantern, received upon the heavens as a screen. Four plates were exposed, when suddenly the full significance of those words was realized, 'Let there be light, and there was light,' for a mighty flood of brilliant light gushed forth, like the rushing, foaming waters of Niagara. The sun came forth like a conqueror from a battle with the Titans, and was greeted with acclamations by the assembled spectators."

A picture of this magnificent spectacle is given in Fig. VII., showing the prominences and corona after a photograph by Professor Eastman, which was taken at the commencement of the totality. The instant the totality began, the corona made its appearance as a light of silvery whiteness, with an exceedingly tender flush of a greenish-violet hue at the extreme edges, and not the slightest change was perceptible during the totality in the color, the outline, or the position of the rays — an observation confirmed by Professor Hough at Mattoon (Illinois), by Gill, and by several others.

The corona appeared to consist of two principal portions: the inner one, next to the sun, was nearly annular, reaching an elevation of about 1', and in color of a pure silvery whiteness; the outer portion consisted of rays, some of which grouped themselves into five star-like points, while the others assumed the appearance of radiations, and were the most sharply defined; the corona was scarcely visible between the prominences *a* and *b*. The star-like rays attained a height equal to *half the diameter of the sun.*

The observations made by several astronomers in India during the eclipse of 1868, and those made by many others in America during that of 1869, and still later those by Lockyer, Janssen, and others in and near the island of Ceylon, in December, 1871, fully justify the conclusion that, independently of the cosmical materials which must exist in the neighborhood of the sun, there exists around this body

FIG. VII.

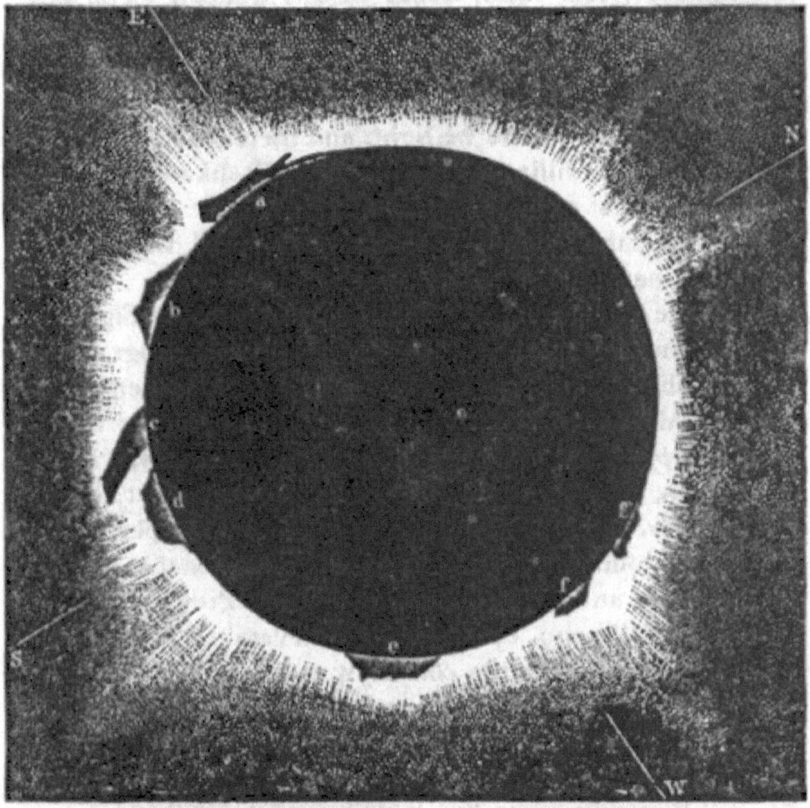

The Corona of the Eclipse of 7th August, 1869, at Des Moines.

an atmosphere very extensive and excessively rare, with hydrogen for its basis. This atmosphere, which undoubtedly forms the outside gaseous envelope of the sun, is fed by the material of the protuberances projected with such violence from the bowels of the photosphere, but is distinguished from the chromosphere and the protuberances by a density enormously less, a lower temperature, and perhaps by the presence of certain different gases.

The prominences are masses of luminous gas, principally luminous hydrogen gas; they envelop the entire surface of the solar body, sometimes in a low stratum extending over exceedingly large tracts of the sun's surface, sometimes in accumulated masses rising at certain localities to a height of more than 80,000 miles.

They are, as respects their first formation, phenomena of eruption. The velocity with which the gaseous matter of the prominences must pass the photosphere must be, in many cases at least, two hundred miles per second, and its initial velocity probably not less than three hundred miles per second. Dense gaseous matter flung out with the hydrogen would probably retain a velocity of, say two hundred and forty miles per second, and reach a height exceeding that indicated by the greatest extension of the radiations observed last December.

The body of the sun, or its light-giving envelope, the photosphere, is completely surrounded by a gaseous envelope, in which hydrogen constitutes the chief element, and which is called the chromosphere. Its mean thickness is between five thousand and seven thousand miles.

The prominences are local accumulations of the *chromosphere*, and therefore pre-eminently of hydrogen gas, which appear to break forth from time to time from the interior of the sun in the form of monster eruptions, forcing their way through the photosphere and chromosphere. As this gas, on effecting a passage, rises with great rapidity, it becomes quickly rarefied in a direction away from the sun's limb.

From the experiments undertaken by Lockyer, Frankland, Wüllner, and Secchi, it appears that *even in the lowest stratum of this gaseous envelope, the pressure is smaller than that of our atmosphere, therefore that the gas of the chromosphere is in a state of greater attenuation.*

Under the chromosphere lies the luminous cloud-like vaporous or nebulous *photosphere*, which contains all the substances, the spectrum lines of which appear as absorption lines in the solar spectrum. These substances — among which iron, magnesium, and sodium are especially prominent — often burst forth in a state of incandescence, and are carried up to a certain distance into the chromosphere, and into the basis of the prominences, though not in general to any considerable elevation.

It is probable that, owing to a continuous decrease in its temperature and density, the chromosphere stretches out into space to a distance far beyond our power of recognition.

Modes of Observing the Prominences in Sunshine. Form of the Prominences.

As early as 1866, Lockyer attempted to observe the prominences in full sunshine by means of a Herschel-Browning spectroscope placed in combination with a telescope. The method he employed, and which he laid before the Royal Society in a special communication, depends on the specific difference between the light of the prominences and that of the sun itself.

The light of an incandescent solid or liquid body which passes through the slit of a spectroscope will be spread out by the prism into a band of greater or less length, and form a *continuous* spectrum.

The light of a gaseous or vaporous body will by the same means, on the contrary, be decomposed into a few only, sometimes even into a very few, bright *lines*.

In the first case, the greater the *length* of the spectrum, the less will be its intensity in comparison with that of the source of light; in the second case, especially when the spectrum consists only of a couple of lines, the intensity of each line is little less than half that of the light itself.

If, therefore, an equal amount of light from two self

luminous bodies, one of which is solid or liquid, and the other gaseous or vaporous, enter the slit of the spectroscope at the same time, the bright lines of the latter will be more brilliant than the color of the corresponding portion of the continuous spectrum.

Now, by *increasing* the number of prisms, the continuous spectrum may become so elongated, and consequently diminished in light, that the once brilliant solar spectrum may be reduced to the verge of visibility, while the same amount of dispersion produces on a spectrum of lines from glowing gas only an increase in the *distance between the lines*, and no considerable diminution of their brilliancy.

The reason why the prominences round the sun's limb cannot be seen through a telescope at any time by screening off the intense light of the sun, is owing to the extreme brilliancy with which the sun illuminates the earth's atmosphere, the particles of which scatter so large an amount of light as quite to overpower the fainter light of the prominences, and prevent them making any sensible impression on the eye.

In a total eclipse of the sun, the light of this atmosphere is so considerably reduced as to allow the larger prominences beyond the limb of the sun to be observed by the unassisted eye. The possibility of reducing the glare of sunlight at any other time without extinguishing the light of the prominences, rests on the circumstance already mentioned, that the light of the sun consists of rays of every color, and therefore produces in a spectroscope of highly dispersive power a long and faint spectrum, while the light of the *prominences*, consisting in general of only three or four kinds of rays, remains even after the greatest dispersive power still concentrated into the same number of lines ($H\alpha$, $H\beta$, $H\gamma$, D_3).

It was on these principles, first announced by Lockyer, that Janssen succeeded, the day after the eclipse of the 18th of August, 1868, in observing the *spectrum* of the prominences in sunshine. That the method he employed was no other than that suggested by Lockyer, is evident from his own communication to the French Academy, dated Calcutta, the 3d of October, 1868, in which he expressed himself as follows: "The principle of the new method rests upon the difference between the spectrum peculiarities of the light of the prominences and that of the photosphere. The light of the photosphere, which is derived from incandescent solid or liquid particles, is incomparably stronger than that of the prominences, which is derived from gases. On this account it has been impossible hitherto to see the prominences, except during a total solar eclipse. By the employment, however, of spectrum analysis, the circumstances of the case may be reversed. *In fact, by the process of analyzation, the light of the sun is dispersed over the whole range of the spectrum, and its intensity becomes considerably lessened. The prominences, on the contrary, furnish only a few detached groups of rays which are bright enough to bear comparison with the corresponding rays of the solar spectrum.* It is for this reason that the *lines* of the prominences may be seen easily in the same field of the spectroscope with the solar spectrum, while the direct images of the prominences are invisible on account of the overpowering light of the sun. Another circumstance very favorable to the new method of observation lies in the fact that the bright lines of the prominences correspond with the dark lines of the solar spectrum: they can, therefore, not only be more easily recognized in the field of the spectroscope along the edges of the solar spectrum, but also detected on the solar spectrum itself, and their traces even followed on the very surface of the sun."

As soon as Janssen and Lockyer had succeeded by this method in observing the *spectrum* of the prominences independently of a total eclipse, it became a question whether it would not be possible not merely to see the lines of the prominences, but also to make their actual forms visible during sunshine.

It was on the principles before mentioned that Lockyer based his plan of observing the spectra of the prominences in full sunlight by means of a telespectroscope (Fig. VIII.).

FIG. VIII.

LOCKYER'S TELESPECTROSCOPE.

For this purpose the slit of a highly dispersive spectroscope, $d\,c\,e\,h$, firmly attached by the rods $a\,a\,b$ to an equatorially mounted telescope L T P, driven by clockwork, is directed perpendicularly on to the edge of the sun's image formed in the telescope. By moving the tube e of the spectroscope from end to end of the spectrum, and setting the focus each time, the bright lines of the prominences may be seen as *prolongations* of the dark lines of the spectrum of the sun's disk on a background of the exceedingly faint spectrum of the earth's atmosphere. In the picture, S is the finder, *g* a handle for moving the telescope in declination, *d* the tube containing the slit, *h* a small telescope for reading the divisions on the micrometer screw head, partly concealed by the rod *a a*.

The telespectroscope is furnished with seven prisms, and it confirmed, after a few trials, the correctness of this view, and he was the first to succeed, without additional mechanical help or the use of colored glasses, in observing the prominences at any time when the sun was visible, and tracing their complete outline.

By the same means Zöllner saw the prominences for the first time on the 1st of July, 1869. He has published the results of his observations, and accompanied them by a series of highly interesting drawings of some of the larger prominences, in which their origin, development, and subsequent disappearance are very clearly exhibited.

When the spectrum of the earth's atmosphere has disappeared in consequence of the *powerful dispersion of the light*, and the portion of the prominence then in the field of view alone is visible through the widely opened slit, the telescope or slit is moved slowly forward, and luminous images of the most wonderful forms flit before the eye, being just as easily observed as during a total solar eclipse. In describing some of these shadow forms, Lockyer writes, "Here one is reminded, by the fleecy, infinitely delicate cloud-films, of an English hedgerow with luxuriant elms; here of a densely intertwined tropical forest, the intimately interwoven branches threading in all directions, the prominences generally expanding as they mount upward, and changing slowly, indeed almost imperceptibly. . . . As a rule, the attachment to the chromosphere is narrow, and is not often single; higher up, the stems, so to speak, intertwine, and the prominence expands and soars upward until it is lost in delicate filaments, which are carried away in floating masses."

The various forms of the prominences may be classified generally into two characteristic groups, very aptly designated by Zöllner as *vaporous* or *cloud-like* forms, and *eruptive* forms.

Slight changes in the form of the prominences may be watched almost without intermission with an open slit; great changes, as a rule, take place only very slowly, or quite imperceptibly. In some cases, however, the change in the form of a prominence is so extraordinary, and occurs with such rapidity, that it can only be ascribed to extremely violent agitation in the upper portions of the solar atmosphere, compared with which the cyclonic storms occasionally agitating the earth's atmosphere sink into insignificance. The observation of such a solar storm has been thus described by Lockyer:—

"On the 14th of March, 1869, about 9 h. 45 m., with a slit tangential to the sun's limb instead of radial, which was its usual position, I observed a fine dense prominence near the sun's equator, on the eastern limb, in which intense action was evidently taking place. At 10 h. 50 m., when the action was slackening, I opened the slit; I saw at once that the dense appearance had all disappeared, and cloud-like filaments had taken its place. At 11 h. 5 m., it was about twenty-seven thousand miles high, and the portion on the left resembled a straight column in a slightly leaning position. I left the Observatory for a few minutes, and on returning, at 11 h. 15 m., I was astonished to find that part of the straight prominence had entirely disappeared; not even the slightest rack appeared in its place: whether it was entirely dissipated, or whether parts of it had been wafted towards the other part, I do not know, although I think the latter explanation the more probable one, as the other part had increased. Fig. IX. shows the prominence as it appeared at the last observation.

FIG. IX.

STORM OBSERVED BY LOCKYER ON THE 14th MARCH, 1859.

Professor C. A. Young, of Dartmouth College, Hanover, N. H., has devoted himself especially to the observation of the forms and variability of the prominences. In the colored plate accompanying this paper are represented some of the forms and the color of the prominences. The one here shown is of the vaporous or cloud-like form, and was observed by Professor Young, October 7, 1869.

The change in the form between the first and second observation will serve to illustrate the motions of the hydrogen flames, and will give the reader some slight idea of the disturbances which are constantly occurring on the surface of the sun. By means of the accompanying scale their height can be easily ascertained. Professor Young has since observed others of a much greater height and magnitude.

As the meteorologist registers many times in a day the conditions of our atmosphere, in the hope that a comparison of the observations may lead to a discovery of the law governing these changes, so has Respighi, Director of the University Observatory at the Campidoglio at Rome, made it his daily task since October, 1869, to observe the entire limb of the sun, when the weather was favorable, including the chromosphere and prominences, and to mark upon a straight line representing the circumference of the sun the position, height, and form of the prominences for each day. By collating these lines or circumferences of the sun one below the other, and crossing them with lines indicating the principal positions, a comprehensive picture is afforded of the distribution of the prominences round the sun's limb, which shows at a glance those regions in which the prominences abound, and those in which they are least frequently to be met with.

By a comparison of the maps already constructed, Respighi has arrived at the following results: —

1. In the polar regions prominences occur only exceptionally. The district from which they are absent lies between north and north-east on the one side, and south and south-west on the other; the portion which is almost entirely without prominences has a semi-diameter of $22\frac{1}{2}°$.

2. The district where the prominences most frequently occur lies between north and north-west, at about $45°$ north latitude, in a region where solar spots are rarely seen.

3. The prominences are, therefore, phenomena quite distinct from the spots; they are probably more intimately connected with the formation of *faculæ*.

4. The various forms of the prominences show that they are not of the nature of *clouds*, which float in an atmosphere in which they are produced by local condensations; they are much more like *eruptions* out of the chromosphere,

Solar Prominence observed by Young 1869·Oct 7 & 8 Pos 70° 80°

Nº 1. Time Oct. 7. 2ʰ 45ᵐ English miles. Nº 2. Time Oct. 8. 1ʰ 50ᵐ 4ʰ

which often spread out of the higher regions, and take the form of bouquets of flowers, some being bent over on one side, and some on the other, and which fall again on to the surface of the chromosphere as rapidly as they rose from it.

5. It appears that *eruptions of hydrogen* take place from the interior of the sun; their form and the extreme rapidity of their motion necessitates the hypothesis of a *repulsive power*, at work either at the surface or in the mass of the sun, which Respighi attributes to electricity, but Faye simply to the action of the intense heat of the photosphere.

On the 28th of September, 1870, Professor Young succeeded for the first time in photographing the prominences on the sun's limb in bright sunshine. This he effected by bringing the blue hydrogen line H γ near G into the middle of the field of the spectroscope, and placing a small photographic camera in connection with the eye-piece of the telescope. As the chemicals employed were those ordinarily used in taking portraits, the requisite time of exposure was three and one half minutes, during which time the image of the prominence suffered a slight displacement on the prepared plate, owing to a want of accuracy in the perfect adjustment of the polar axis. Still, however, the various forms of the prominences could be clearly discerned in the photograph, which was half an inch in diameter, so that the possibility of photographing the prominences has been proved by Young's experiment.

Measurement of the Direction and Speed of the Gas-streams in the Sun.

One of the most glorious triumphs of spectrum analysis — surpassing, perhaps, in splendor all its other wonderful achievements — is the discovery that, by means of accurate measurements, undertaken with the best instruments, of the position, or rather of the small *displacement in the position* of the spectrum lines of a star or other source of light, — a prominence, for instance, — it is possible to ascertain whether this luminous body be approaching us or receding from us, and at what speed it is travelling.

The pitch of a musical tone depends, as is well known, upon the number of impulses which the ear receives from the air in a given time (p. 74). Now, as a tone rises in pitch the greater the number of air vibrations which strike the tympanum in a second, so must a sound ascend in tone if we rapidly approach it, and fall in pitch if we recede from it. The truth of this supposition may be fully proved by the whistle of a railway engine in rapid motion. To an observer standing still, the pitch of the tone rises on the rapid approach of the locomotive, although the same note is sounded, and falls again as the engine travels away.

As the various tones of sound depend on the rapidity of the air vibrations, so the varieties of color are regulated by the number of ether vibrations (p. 77). If, therefore, a luminous object — as, for instance, the glowing hydrogen of a prominence — be *receding* rapidly from us, fewer waves of ether will strike the optic nerve in a second than if it were stationary. If the difference in the number of ether waves be sufficiently great to be perceived by the eye, then each color of the glowing gas must sink in the scale of the spectrum, — that is to say, incline more towards the red. The individual colored rays will not then, in the prismatic decomposition of the light, occur in the same place of the spectrum in which they would have appeared had the light been stationary; they will all be displaced somewhat towards the *red*.

The converse takes place when the luminous body is rapidly approaching us: the number of ether vibrations received by the eye is then increased beyond what it would be if the source of light were stationary; in the prismatic analysis of the light, the colored rays will be found likewise to have changed their place in the scale of the spectrum, and taken a position in accordance with their increased refrangibility, suffering a general displacement towards the *violet*.

When it is remembered that the number of ether waves in red light is at least 480 billion, and in violet 800 billion in a second, and that moreover the wave length of the greenish-blue light (H β), situated at the spot marked F in the solar spectrum, is only 485 millionth of a millimetre, and that instruments of sufficient delicacy to measure these minute quantities are required for this purpose, there will be little danger of under-estimating the extreme difficulty connected with observations of this displacement in the colors of the spectrum. Indeed, these observations would scarcely be possible, were it not that in the dark lines crossing the spectra of the sun and fixed stars, the places of some of which may be accurately ascertained, we have fixed positions in the spectrum, the degree of refrangibility or wave-length of which may be determined beforehand, both for the sun and terrestrial substances, and also for the stars or other sources of light supposed to be at rest.

Fig. X., which is from a drawing by Lockyer, shows clearly what remarkable changes take place in the dark line

FIG. X.

Displacement of the F-line; Velocity of the Gas-streams in the Sun.

F when the spectroscope is directed to a solar spot in the middle of the sun. The F-line, which, as a rule, is sharply defined at the edges, appears in some places not merely as a bright line, but as a bright and dark line twisted together, in which parts it suffers the greatest displacement towards the red. When this occurs, there is frequently also a bright line to be seen on the violet side. In small solar spots, this line sometimes breaks off suddenly, or spreads out immediately before its termination in a globular form; over the bright faculæ of a spot (the bridges) the line is often altogether wanting, or else it is reversed, and appears as a bright line.

The same phenomena are exhibited also by the red C-line (H α), though as the greenish-blue F-line (H β) is by an equal increase of pressure much more sensitive with regard to expansion than the red line is, and exhibits with greater distinctness the changes that have been already described, it is better adapted to observations of this kind.

All these expansions, twistings, and displacements of the F-line result from a change in the wave-length of the greenish-blue light emitted by the moving masses of incandescent hydrogen gas in the sun. The middle of this line, when it is well defined, corresponds to a wave-length of 485 millionth of a millimetre, yet it is possible, by means of Ångström's maps of the solar spectrum, to measure a displacement of this line when the wave-length has only changed as much as $\frac{1}{10,000,000}$ of a millimetre, and, inversely, it is also possible to read off at once, by the measured displacement of the F-line, the corresponding amount which the wave-length of the greenish-blue hydrogen light has lengthened or shortened, to ten millionth of a millimetre. In observing a prominence, if the F-line were to be displaced from its normal place in the solar spectrum $\frac{1}{10,000,000}$ of a millimetre, the light would be approaching the eye of the observer, and an eruption of gas be *ascending* at the spot observed in the middle of the sun, and would be approaching the earth at the rate of thirty-six miles per second.

If the F-line were to suffer an equal displacement to the left, that is to say, towards the red, the wave-length of the greenish-blue hydrogen light would then be lengthened; the gas would therefore be moving away from the earth at the same rate of thirty-six miles in a second, and the stream of gas be sinking down to the surface of the sun.

Fig. XI. shows the displacement which occurs when a cyclone takes place on the sun's surface. Such a circular storm or cyclone was observed by Lockyer on the sun's limb, on the 14th of March, 1869. With the first setting of

MOVEMENT OF A GAS-VORTEX IN THE SUN.

the slit, the image of the bright F-line (H β) in the chromosphere appeared in the spectroscope, as in No. 1; a slight alteration of the slit gave in succession the pictures 2 and 3. There occurred also a simultaneous displacement of the bright F-line towards both the red and violet—a sign that at that place on the sun a portion of the hydrogen was moving towards the earth, while another portion was going in an opposite direction away from the earth towards the sun, and thus the whole action of the gas in motion resembled that of a whirlwind.

By means of the distances from the normal dark F-line which are taken from Ångström's maps, Lockyer found that the furthest displacement of the bright F-line corresponded to a shortening of the wave-length that indicated a velocity in the stream of gas of at least one hundred and forty-seven miles in a second in the direction from the sun towards the earth.

These spectroscopic observations receive an additional interest when taken in connection with those made with the telescope. On the 21st of April, 1869, Lockyer observed a spot in the neighborhood of the sun's limb. At 7 h. 30 m., a prominence showing great activity appeared in the field of view. The lines of hydrogen were remarkably brilliant, and as the spectrum of the spot was visible in the same field, it could be seen that the prominence was advancing towards the spot. The violence of the eruption was so great as to carry up a quantity of metallic vapors out of the photosphere in a manner not previously observed. High up in the flame of hydrogen floated a cloud of magnesium vapor. At 8 h. 30 m. the eruption was over; but an hour later another eruption began, and the new prominence displayed a motion of extreme rapidity. Whilst this was taking place, the hydrogen lines at the side of the spot nearest to the earth were suddenly changed into bright lines, and expanded so remarkably as to give undoubted evidence of the occurrence of a cyclonic storm.

The sun was photographed at Kew on the same day at 10 h. 55 m.; the picture showed clearly that great disturbances had taken place in the photosphere in the neighborhood of the spot observed by Lockyer. In a second photograph, taken at 4 h. 1 m., the sun's limb appeared as if torn away just at the place where the spectroscope had revealed a rotatory storm.

Who could have dreamed, ten years ago, that we should so soon attain such an insight into the processes of creation? And yet, great though the results of spectrum analysis already are, they are but a tithe of the numerous questions which this branch of discovery has opened up, — questions of such number and magnitude, that many generations of men will pass away before they are all satisfactorily answered.

Spectra of the Moon and Planets.

Since the planets and their satellites do not emit light of their own, but shine only by the reflected light of the sun, their spectra are the same as the solar spectrum, and any differences that may be perceived can arise only from the changes the sunlight may undergo by reflection from the surfaces of these bodies, or by its passage through their atmospheres.

The observations of Huggins and Miller, as well as Janssen, agree in establishing the complete accordance of the lunar spectrum with that of the sun. In all the various portions of the moon's disk brought under observation, no difference could be perceived in the dark lines of the spectrum, either in respect of their number or relative intensity. From this entire absence of any special absorption lines, it must be concluded that there is no atmosphere in the moon, — a conclusion previously arrived at from the circumstance that during an occultation no refraction is perceived on the moon's limb when a star disappears behind the disk.

The spectra of the planets Venus, Mars, Jupiter, and Saturn are also characterized by the Fraunhofer lines peculiar to the solar light, but contain, in addition, the absorption lines which are known to be telluric lines, and are evidence of the presence of an atmosphere containing aqueous vapor.

The spectrum of Jupiter, which has been recently examined by Browning with a spectroscope attached to his $12\frac{1}{2}$-inch reflector, is not of sufficient brilliancy to allow of its being observed or measured with extreme accuracy. Notwithstanding the great brilliancy with which this planet shines in the heavens, its spectrum is not so bright as that of a star of the second magnitude; this is owing to the brightness being more apparent than real, and arises from the large size of the disk compared with a star, and from the light being reflected, and not original.

The comparatively faint spectrum of Saturn has been examined by Huggins, who observed in it some of the lines characteristic of Jupiter's spectrum. These lines are less clearly seen in the light of the ring than in that of the ball, whence it may be concluded that the light from the ring suffers less absorption than does the light from the planet itself. The observations of Janssen, which have been supported by Secchi, have since shown that aqueous vapor is probably present both in Jupiter and Saturn. Secchi has further discovered some lines in the spectrum of Saturn which are not coincident with any of the telluric lines, nor with any of the lines of the solar spectrum produced by the aqueous vapor of the earth's atmosphere. It is not improbable, therefore, that the atmosphere of Saturn may contain gases or vapors which do not exist in that of our earth.

The spectrum of Uranus, which has been investigated by Secchi, appears to be of a very remarkable character. It consists mainly of two broad black bands, one in the greenish-blue, but not coincident with the F-line, and the other in the green, near the line E. A little beyond the band the spectrum disappears altogether, and shows a blank space extending entirely over the yellow to the red, where there is again a faint re-appearance of light. The spectrum is therefore such a one as would be produced were all the yellow rays extinguished from the light of the sun. The dark sodium line D occurs, as is well known, in the part of the spectrum occupied by this broad, non-luminous space: is this extraordinary phenomenon, therefore, to be ascribed to the influence of this metal, or is the planet Uranus, which has a spectrum differing so greatly from that of the sun, self-luminous? Has the planet not yet attained that degree of consistency possessed by the nearer planets, which shine only by the sun's light, and, as the photometric observations of Zöllner lead us to suppose is possible, is still in that process of condensation and subsequent development through which the earth has already passed? These are questions to which, at present, we can furnish no reply, and the problem can only be solved by additional observations of the strange characteristics exhibited by this spectrum.

While Jupiter and his satellites, with a power of 350, give a sharply defined image, the disk of Neptune, with the same power, ceases to be well defined, and appears with a nebulous edge. From this it may be inferred that the planet is surrounded by a dense mist of considerable extent, the chemical nature of which has yet to be discovered, or else that, like Jupiter, Saturn, and Uranus, it has not yet attained that degree of density which must necessarily precede the formation of a solid surface.

Spectra of the Fixed Stars.

The fixed stars, though immensely more remote, and less conspicuous in brightness than the moon and planets, yet from the fact of their being *original sources of light*, furnish us with fuller indications of their nature. In all ages, and among every people, the stars have been the object of admiring wonder, and not unfrequently of superstitious adoration. The greatest investigators and the deepest thinkers who have devoted themselves to the study of the stars, have felt a longing to know more of these sparkling mysteries.

The telescope has been appealed to, but in vain, for in the largest instruments the stars remained diskless, never appearing more than as brilliant points. The stars have indeed been represented as *suns*, each surrounded by a dependent group of planets, but this opinion rested only upon a possible analogy, for of the *peculiar nature* of these points of light, and of what substances they are composed, the telescope yields us no information. Spectrum analysis alone can disclose to us this much-coveted knowledge, as it gives us the means of reading, in the light emitted by these heavenly bodies, the indications of their true nature and physical constitution. In this light we possess a telegraphic communication between the stars and our earth; the spectroscope is the telegraph, the spectrum lines are individually the letters of the alphabet, their united assemblage as a spectrum forms the telegram. It is not, however, easy to comprehend this language of the stars, but through the indefatigable labors of Secchi, Huggins, and Miller, most of the bright stars, the nebulæ, and some of the comets have been investigated by spectrum analysis, and valuable evidence obtained as to their physical constitution.

As the spectra of the stars bear in general a marked resemblance to the spectrum of the sun, being continuous, and crossed by dark lines, there is every reason for applying Kirchhoff's theory also to the fixed stars, and for accepting the same explanation of these similar phenomena that we have already accepted for the sun. By the supposition that the vaporous *incandescent* photosphere of a star contains or is surrounded by heated vapors, which absorb the same rays of light which they would emit when self-luminous, we may discover from the dark lines in the stellar spectra the substances which are contained in the photosphere or atmosphere of each star. In order to ascertain this with certainty, the dark lines must be compared with the bright lines of terrestrial substances volatilized in the electric spark; and the complete coincidence of the characteristic bright lines of a terrestrial substance with the same number of dark lines in the stellar spectrum, would justify the conclusion that this substance is present in the atmosphere of the star — a conclusion that gains all the more in certainty, the greater the number of lines coincident in the two spectra.

The fact that certain stars possess an atmosphere of aqueous vapor has been observed both by Janssen and Secchi. They belong, for the most part, to the class of red and yellow stars, and in their spectra, as might be supposed, the lines of luminous hydrogen are wanting. As early as 1864, Janssen had remarked the existence of an atmosphere of aqueous vapor in the star Antares; and after a more complete investigation of the spectrum of steam in 1866, and further observations of stellar spectra, made after the total solar eclipse of 1868 in the remarkably dry air of the heights of Sikkim (Himalaya), he could no longer doubt that there are many stars surrounded by a similar atmosphere. Notwithstanding the dry condition of the air, the lines of aqueous vapor were more strongly marked in the spectra of these stars, as seen from the heights of the Himalaya, than had been observed previously — a phenomenon which cannot be ascribed to the absorption of the earth's atmosphere, and must therefore be due to that of the star.

From all the observations thus far made, it may be concluded that at least the brightest stars have a physical constitution similar to that of our sun. Their light radiates, like that of the sun, from matter in a state of intense incandescence, and passes, in like manner, through an atmosphere of absorptive vapors. Notwithstanding this general conformity of structure, there is yet a great difference in the constitution of individual stars; the grouping of the various elements is peculiar and characteristic for each star, and we must suppose that even these individual peculiarities are in necessary accordance with the special object of the star's existence, and its adaptation to the animal life of the planetary worlds by which it is surrounded.

Color of the Stars. — Double Stars and their Spectra.

In a transparent atmosphere, especially in a southern clime, the stars do not all appear with the white brilliancy of the diamond: here and there the eye discovers richly-colored gems, sparkling on the sombre robe of night, in every shade of red, green, blue, and violet; and the astronomer, enabled by his powerful telescope to investigate the faintest objects, is lost in wonder over the variety of these colors, and their remarkable distribution in the starry heavens. This play of color is most conspicuous in the *double stars*, so called from their consisting of two or more suns, kept together by the bond of mutual attraction, and revolving in orbits according to their mass, either one around the other or both round a common centre of gravity. To the naked eye their appearance is that of a single star, on account of their close proximity; but on the application of sufficient magnifying power, they are found to be constituted of three, four, or more suns in intimate connection: such a system is to be found in the beautiful constellation of Orion (in the Sword), consisting of sixteen stars, where to the unassisted eye there seems but one. In several of these double stars, the number of which already exceeds six thousand, it has been possible to calculate the time of revolution of the small star. The period of one in the Great Bear has been found to be sixty years; of another, in Virgo, five hundred and thirteen years; and of γ Leonis twelve hundred years.

A peculiar interest attaches to double stars from their great diversity of color, which occasioned Sir John Herschel to remark, in describing a cluster in the Southern Cross, that it resembled a splendid ornament composed of the richest jewels. While the majority of single stars shine with a white light, but sometimes with a yellow, and even occasionally with a red hue, in double stars the companion is almost always blue, green, or red, thus contrasting with the white light of the larger or central star.

It has long been a subject of inquiry whence these colors arise. It has been supposed that they were complementary colors, and therefore that they were not inherent in the stars, but dependent on an optical illusion similar to that produced by looking upon a white wall immediately after gazing at the sun, when the wall appears covered with violet spots. But the simple expedient of covering the central star in the telescope suffices to show the incorrectness of this supposition; for the color of the small star remains unaffected by its separation from the light of the larger one. Zöllner, to whom we are indebted for a masterly work on light and the physical constitution of the heavenly bodies, was the first to express the idea that, as all known substances, in their transition from a state of incandescence to that of a lower temperature, pass through the stage of red heat, so the fixed stars, in their process of development from the condition of glowing gas through the period of an incandescent liquid state, and the subsequent development of floating scoriæ, or gradual formation of a cold, non-luminous surface, must, together with the gradual diminution of their light, be also subject to a change of color. For many colored stars, especially for the so-called *new* stars, in which the color has been known to sink in the scale from white to yellow and to red, this conjecture of Zöllner's has a high degree of probability; but that other circumstances must exercise an influence also on the color of stars, is proved by a change of color having been observed to take place in the opposite direction, — that is, from red to white, — of which, among other stars, we have an example in Sirius, regarded by the ancients as a red star, and which is now considered as a type of the white stars, as well as in Capella, which formerly was red, and now shines with a pale blue light. Huggins and Miller have discovered, by means of the spectroscope, that the color of a star not only depends upon the degree of incandescence of the intensely hot liquid or solid nucleus, but also upon the kind of absorptive power its atmosphere may exert upon the light emitted by the glowing nucleus.

As the source of stellar light, remarks Huggins, is incandescent solid or liquid matter, it appears very probable that at the time of its emission the light of all stars is alike *white*. The colors in which we see them must therefore be produced by certain changes which the light has undergone since its emission. It is further obvious that if the dark absorption lines are more numerous, or more strongly marked in some parts of the spectrum than in others, then the peculiar colors of those places will be subdued in tone, and in any case will appear relatively weaker than in those parts of the spectrum where the absorption lines are much less numerous. While in this way certain colors would be partially extinguished from the spectrum, the remaining colors, being unaffected, would predominate, and give their own tints to the originally white light of the star.

The colors of the stars are, therefore, without doubt produced by the vapors of certain substances contained in their atmosphere; and as the chemical constitution of the atmosphere of a star depends upon the elements of which the star itself is composed, and upon its temperature, it would be possible to ascertain the chief constituents of these small telescopic worlds, if the position of the dark absorption lines could be determined with accuracy, or if these lines could be compared with the spectrum lines of terrestrial elements.

Variable Stars.

Among the fixed stars there are several which vary, from time to time, in brightness, as compared with neighboring stars; their light increases or diminishes, and alternates, in some cases, from the brilliancy even of a star of the first magnitude to complete invisibility. In some, this change of brightness takes place as a constant, very slow and regular diminution of light; in others, there appears an almost sudden increase and decrease of brilliancy; while with others, again, the change takes place within regularly recurring periods. The *period* of variability is, therefore, the time elapsing between the two successive seasons of greatest brilliancy.

Of all variable stars, Mira Ceti is perhaps the most interesting, since, at its maximum brightness, it equals a star of the first or second magnitude. Scarcely less interesting is β Persei, which, for two days thirteen hours and a half, shines with the brightness of a star of the second magnitude, then suddenly decreases in light, and sinks down, in three hours and a half, to a star of the fourth magnitude; its light then again increases, and in a similar period of three hours and a half regains its original brilliancy. All these changes recur regularly in the space of less than three days, during which the star always remains visible to the naked eye.

Whence comes this variation in the light of a star? Zöllner, with great acuteness, and supported by numerous observations of these changes of brightness, offers a simple and unconstrained explanation, in supposing the cause to lie in the configuration and distribution of dark masses of scoriæ, which form on the red-hot liquid body of the star in the process of cooling, and which, in consequence of the star's rotation on its axis, and the centrifugal force thus arising, would take certain definite courses on the surface of the star in a manner analogous to that which may be observed with floating icebergs on our earth. As a consequence of this peculiar relative motion, the dark masses of scoriæ would arrange themselves in a fixed order, and would produce on the surface of the star an unequal distribution of red-hot luminous matter, and accumulations of non-luminous scoriæ.

It has recently been remarked by Secchi that the spectrum of the nucleus of a solar spot bears a close resemblance to that given by several red stars, such as α Orionis, Antares, Aldebaran, ο Ceti. A series of dark bands and stripes, as represented in the spectrum of α Orionis, are present equally in the spectrum of a solar spot as in the spectra of the above named red stars, which leads to the supposition that the red color of these stars arises from the same cause that produces the absorption bands in the spectrum of the solar spot. As nearly all these stars are variable, it is not improbable that they are also subject to spots which occur with a certain degree of regularity, as the solar spots have been proved to do. The period of variability in the light would then depend upon the period of the formation of the spots, in the same way as our sun appears as a variable star, of which the period of variation in the light coincides with the regular recurrence of the spots.

New or Temporary Stars.

Among the variable stars must also be reckoned those which, from time to time, but only at exceedingly long intervals, have suddenly flamed forth in the sky and disappeared again after a longer or shorter interval, and which always excite the greatest wonder and interest, not only from the rarity of their appearance, but also from the mighty revolutions in space which they announce. According to Humboldt, only twenty-one such stars have been recorded in the space of two thousand years, — from 134 B. C. to 1848 A. D., — the most remarkable of which was that observed by Tycho Brahe (1572) in Cassiopeiæ, which surpassed both Sirius and Jupiter, and even rivalled Venus in brilliancy, but disappeared after seventeen months, without leaving a trace visible to the naked eye;* and that seen by Kepler (1604) in the right foot of Ophiuchus, which excelled Jupiter, but did not quite equal Venus, in brightness, and at the end of fifteen months was visible only by means of the telescope. Two similar stars, which have appeared in recent times, — one observed by Hind, in 1848, and another seen in the Northern Crown, in 1866, — though they soon lost their ephemeral glory, still continue visible as stars of the tenth and ninth magnitude. A characteristic peculiarity of these temporary stars is, that they nearly all flash out at once with a degree of brilliancy exceeding, in some cases, even stars of the first magnitude, and that they have not been observed, at least with the naked eye, to increase gradually in brightness.

Are we to suppose that these so-called *new* stars are really

---

* The telescope was not invented until thirty-seven years after this date.

new creations, as Tycho Brahe believed, and that those that have disappeared are really annihilated or burned out? Can we suppose, with Riccioli, that these heavenly bodies are luminous only on one side, which by a sudden semi-revolution the Creator, at the appointed time, has turned towards us? The first supposition has been set aside by later observations, which have shown, by the help of maps, that a small star had already existed precisely in the place where the new star burst forth; the other view is too absurd to deserve, in these days, any further consideration. The star observed by Tycho, as well as that one seen by Kepler, are still visible. If, therefore, the sudden bursting forth of a star in the heavens does not denote the creation of a new star, nor its gradual disappearance indicate its complete annihilation, we may well suppose that both phenomena are the successive effects of a violent outbreak of fire taking place in the star, either in the form of an eruption of the internal red-hot liquid matter, and its suffusion over the surface, or of the ignition of gigantic streams of gas forcing their way from the interior. While such an occurrence would raise the star to a state of extreme incandescence, and cause it to emit an intense light for some time, the cooling subsequent to this combustion would ensue more or less rapidly, and the brightness consequently diminish in quick progression, until, in certain conditions, the star would cease to be visible.

Fortunately for science, such an occurrence has taken place since spectrum analysis has been so successfully applied to the examination of the heavenly bodies. On the night of the 12th of May, 1866, a new star, brighter than one of the second magnitude, was observed at Tuam, by Mr. John Birmingham, in the constellation Corona Borealis. On the following night it was seen by the French engineer, Courbebaisse, at Rochefort, and was observed a few hours earlier at Athens by the astronomer Julius Schmidt, who expressly declares that the new star could not have been visible before eleven o'clock on the night of the 12th of May, as he had been observing with his comet-seeker the star R Coronæ, and while sweeping for some time in its neighborhood for meteors, could not have failed to notice the new star, if it had been then visible. On the same night (13th of May) the light of the star sensibly decreased, and by the 16th of May it had become only of the fourth magnitude. Its brightness then waned somewhat rapidly: it decreased from 4.9 on the 17th to 5.3 on the 18th, and from 5.7 on the 19th to 6.2 on the 20th, till, by the end of the month, it had become a star of the ninth magnitude.

Argelander observed the star on the 18th of May, 1855, and on the 31st of March, 1856, and on both occasions had classed the star as between the ninth and tenth magnitudes.

Huggins was informed by Birmingham of his discovery on the 14th of May, and was thus enabled, on the 15th inst., in conjunction with Miller, to examine the spectrum of this star when it had not fallen much below the third magnitude. The result of this investigation is as follows.

The spectrum of the star was very remarkable, and showed clearly that there were two distinct sources of light, each producing a separate spectrum, — one a continuous spectrum, crossed by dark lines similar to that given by the sun and other stars, while the other consists of *four bright* lines, which, from their great brilliancy, stand in bold relief upon the dark background of the first spectrum.

The principal spectrum traversed by dark lines shows the presence of a photosphere of incandescent matter, probably solid or liquid, which is surrounded by an atmosphere of cooler vapors, giving rise by absorption to the dark lines. This absorption spectrum contains two strong dark bands, of less refrangibility than the D-line of the solar spectrum; a group of fine lines stretches from them close up to D, while one fine line is quite coincident with D. Up to this point, the constitution of this object is analogous to that of the sun and the stars; but the star has also a spectrum consisting of bright lines, which denotes the presence of a second source of light, which, from the nature of the spectrum, is undoubtedly an intensely luminous gas.

Huggins compared the spectrum of the star on the 17th of May with the spectrum of hydrogen gas produced by means of the induction spark through a Geissler's tube, and found that the strongest of the stellar lines 2 was coincident with the greenish-blue line H β of hydrogen gas. Apparently, also, the line 1 in the red coincided with the H α-line of hydrogen, but owing to the want of brilliancy of the line, the coincidence could not be ascertained with the same degree of certainty. The great brilliancy of these lines, compared with the parts of the continuous spectrum where they occur, proves that the luminous gas was at a higher temperature than the photosphere of the star.

These facts, taken in connection with the suddenness of the outburst of light in the star, and the immediate very rapid decline in its brightness from the second down to the eighth magnitude, have led to the hypothesis already alluded to, that, in consequence of some internal convulsion, enormous quantities of hydrogen and other gases were evolved, which, in combining with some other elements, ignited on the surface of the star, and thus enveloped the whole body suddenly in a sheet of flame. The ignited hydrogen gas, in its combination with some other element, produced the light characterized by the two bright bands in the red and green; the remaining bright lines, among which those of oxygen might have been expected, were not coincident with any of the lines of this gas. The burning hydrogen gas must also have greatly increased the heat of the solid matter of the photosphere, and brought it into a state of more intense incandescence and luminosity, which may explain how the formerly faint star could so suddenly assume such remarkable brilliancy. As the liberated hydrogen gas became exhausted, the flame gradually abated, and with the consequent cooling the photosphere became less vivid, and the star returned to its original condition.

Robert Meyer and H. J. Klein have expressed the opinion that the sudden blazing out of a star might be occasioned by the violent precipitation of some great mass, perhaps of a planet, upon a fixed star, by which the momentum of the falling mass would be changed into molecular motion, or, in other words, into heat and light. It might even be supposed that the star in Corona, through its motion in space, may have come in contact with one of the nebulæ, which traverse in great numbers the realms of space in every direction, and which, from their gaseous condition, must possess a high temperature. Such a collision would necessarily set the star on a blaze, and occasion the most vehement ignition of its hydrogen.

It must not be forgotten that light, though an extremely quick messenger, yet occupies a certain time in coming to us from a star. The speed of light is one hundred and eighty-five thousand miles in a second. The distance of the nearest fixed star (α Centauri) is about sixteen billion miles, so that light takes about three years to travel from this star to us. The great physical convulsion which was observed in the star in Corona, in the year 1866, was therefore an event which had really taken place long before that period, at a time, no doubt, when spectrum analysis, to which we are indebted for the information we obtained on the subject, was yet quite unknown.

The discoveries made by means of spectrum analysis, connected with at least three classes of heavenly bodies, still remain to be reviewed, and will form the basis of another paper of this series, which will be entitled Nebulæ, Comets, and Meteors.

6. Nebulæ, Comets, Meteoric Showers,

And the Revelations of the Spectroscope regarding them.

Spectra of Nebulæ.

WE now come to treat of the remotest realms of the Universe, those regions of stellar clusters and nebulæ which can only be reached by means of the most powerful telescopes. When the starry heavens are viewed through a telescope of moderate power, a great number of stellar clusters and faint nebulous forms are revealed against the dark background of the sky, which might be taken at first sight for passing clouds, but which, by their unchanging forms and persistent appearance, are proved to belong to the heavenly bodies, though possessing a character widely differing from the point-like images of ordinary stars. Sir William Herschel was able, with his gigantic forty-foot telescope, to resolve many of these nebulæ into clusters of stars, and found them to consist of vast groups of individual suns, in which thousands of fixed stars may be clearly separated and counted, but which are so far removed from us that we are unable to perceive their distance one from the other, though that may really amount to many millions of miles, and their light, with a low magnifying power, seems to come from a large, faintly-luminous mass. But all nebulæ were not resolvable with this telescope, and in proportion as such nebulæ were resolved into clusters of stars, new nebulæ appeared which resisted a power of six thousand, and suggested to this astute investigator the theory that, besides the many thousand apparent nebulæ which reveal themselves to us as a complete and separate system of worlds, there are also thousands of real nebulæ in the Universe, composed of *primeval cosmical matter, out of which future worlds were to be fashioned.*

Lord Rosse, by means of a telescope of fifty-two feet focus, of his own construction, was able to resolve into clusters of stars many of the nebulæ not resolved by Herschel; but there were still revealed to the eye, thus carried farther into space, new nebulæ beyond the power even of this gigantic telescope to resolve.

Telescopes failed, therefore, to solve the question whether the unresolved nebulæ are portions of the primeval matter out of which the existing stars have been formed; they leave us in uncertainty as to whether these nebulæ are masses of luminous gas, which, in the lapse of ages, would pass through the various stages of incandescent liquid (the sun and fixed stars), of scoriæ or gradual formation of a cold and non-luminous surface (the earth and planets), and finally of complete gelation and torpidity (the moon), or whether they exist as a complete and separate system of worlds; telescopes have only widened the problem, and have neither simplified nor solved its difficulties.

That which was beyond the power of the most gigantic telescopes has been accomplished by that apparently insignificant, but really delicate, and almost infinitely sensitive instrument, the spectroscope. We are indebted to it for being able to say with certainty that luminous nebulæ *actually exist as isolated bodies in space*, and that these bodies are *luminous masses of gas*.

The spectroscope, in combination with the telescope, affords means for ascertaining, even now, some of the phases through which the sun and planets have passed in their process of development or transition from masses of luminous nebulæ to their present condition.

Great variety is observed in the forms of the nebulæ: while some are chaotic and irregular, and sometimes highly fantastic, others exhibit the pure and beautiful forms of a curve, a crescent, a globe, or a circle.

The largest and most irregular of all the nebulæ is that in the constellation of Orion (Fig. XII.). It is situated rather below the three stars of second magnitude composing the central part of that magnificent constellation, and is visible to the naked eye. It is extremely difficult to execute even a tolerably correct drawing of this nebula; but it appears, from the various drawings, made at different times, that a

Fig. XII.
South.

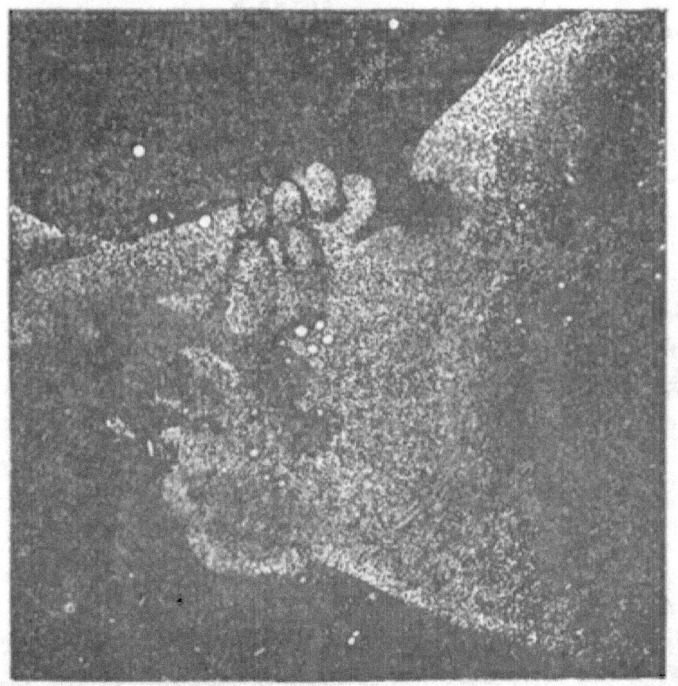

North.

Central and most brilliant portion of the great Nebula in the Sword-handle of Orion, as observed by Sir John Herschel in his 20-foot Reflector at Feldhausen, Cape of Good Hope (1834 to 1837).

change is taking place in the form and position of the brightest portions. Fig. XII. represents the central and brightest part of the nebula. Four bright stars, forming a trapezium, are situated in it, one of which only is visible to the naked eye. The nebula surrounding these stars has a flaky appearance, and is of a greenish-white color; single portions form long curved streaks, stretching out in a radiating manner from the middle and bright parts.

The interest aroused by these irregular and chaotic nebulous forms is still further increased by the phenomena of the spiral or convoluted nebulæ with which the giant telescopes of Lord Rosse and Mr. Bond have made us further acquainted. As a rule, there streams out from one or more centres of luminous matter innumerable curved nebulous streaks, which recede from the centre in a spiral form, and finally lose themselves in space.

Fig. XIII. represents the most remarkable of all the spiral nebulæ, which is situated in the constellation Canes Venatici.

Fig. XIII.

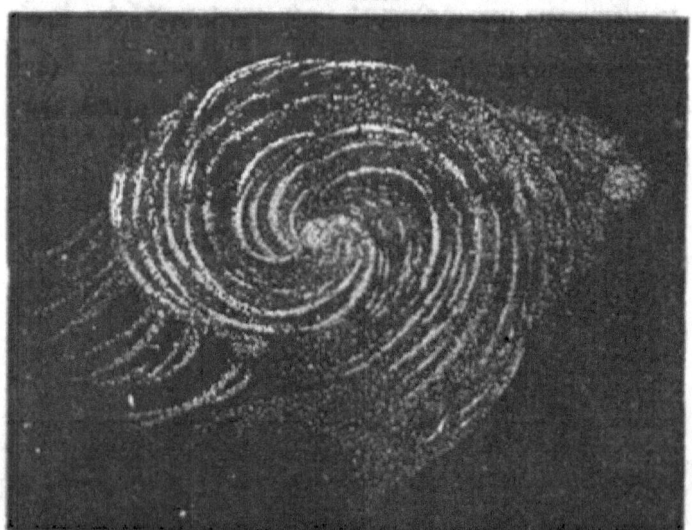

SPIRAL NEBULA IN CANES VENATICI.

It is hardly conceivable that a system of such a nebulous form could exist without internal motion. The bright nucleus, as well as the streaks curving round it in the same direction, seem to indicate an accumulation of matter towards the centre, with a gradual increase of density, and a rotatory movement. But if we combine with this motion the supposition of an opposing medium, it is difficult to harmonize

Fig. XIV.

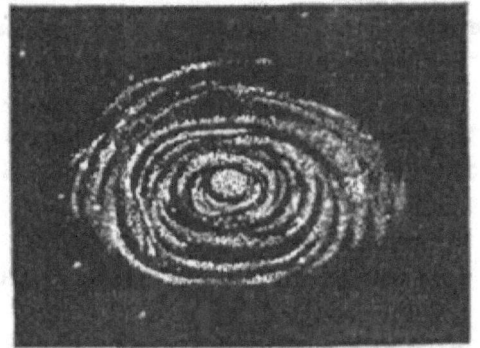

TRANSITION FROM THE SPIRAL TO THE ANNULAR FORM.

such a system with the known laws of statics. Accurate measures are, therefore, of the highest interest for the pur-

Fig. XV.

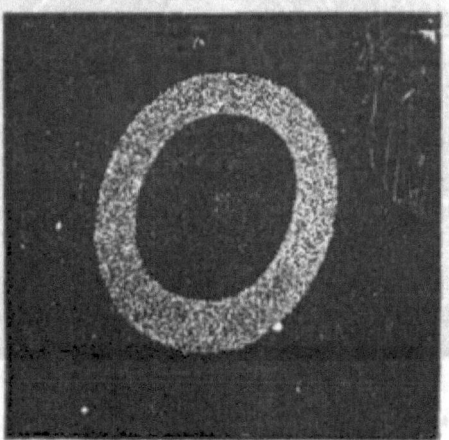

ANNULAR NEBULA IN LYRA.

pose of showing whether actual rotation or other changes are taking place in these nebulæ; but, unfortunately, they are rendered extremely difficult and uncertain by the want of outline, and by the remarkable faintness of these nebulous objects.

The transition state from the spiral to the annular form is shown in such nebulæ as the one represented in Fig. XIV.; and they then pass into the simple or compound annular nebula, of which a type is given in Fig. XV.

The space within most of these elliptic rings is not perfectly dark, but is occupied either by a diffused faint nebulous light, as in Fig. XV., or, as in most cases, by a bright nucleus, round which sometimes one ring, sometimes several, are disposed in various forms.

Those nebulæ which appear with tolerably sharply-defined

FIG. XVI.

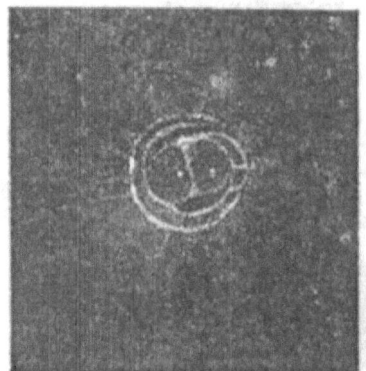

Planetary Nebula with two Stars.

FIG. XVII.

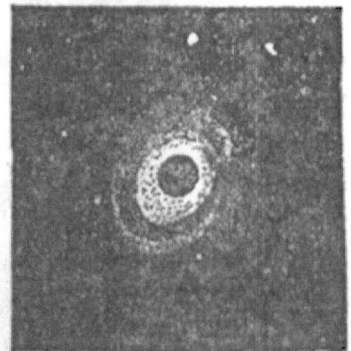

Planetary Nebula.

edges, in the form of a circle or slight ellipse, seem to belong to a much higher stage of development. From their resemblance to those planets which shine with a pale or bluish light, they have been called *planetary* nebulæ; in form, however, they vary considerably, some of them being spiral and some annular. Some of these planetary nebulæ are represented in Figs. XVI. and XVII. The first has two central stars or nuclei, each surrounded by a dark space, beyond which the spiral streaks are disposed; the second is without a nucleus, but shows a well-defined ring of light.

The highest type of nebulæ are certainly the stellar nebulæ, in which a tolerably well defined bright star is surrounded by a completely round disk, or faint atmosphere of light, which sometimes fades away gradually into space, at other times terminates abruptly, with a sharp edge. Fig. XVIII. exhibits one of the most striking of these very remarkable stellar nebulæ. It is a veritable star of the eighth magnitude, and is not nebulous, but is surrounded by a

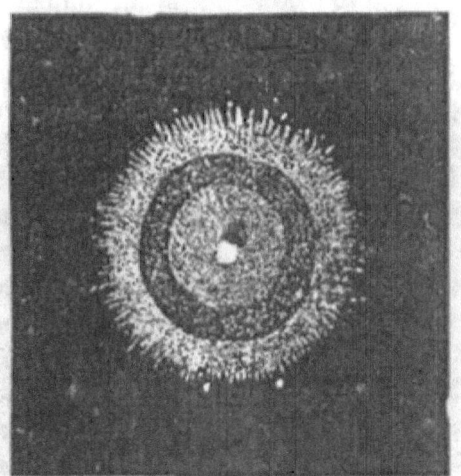

Fig. XVIII.

STELLAR NEBULA.

bright luminous atmosphere perfectly concentric. To the right of the star is a small dark space, such as often occurs in these nebulæ, indicating, perhaps, an opening in the surrounding atmosphere.

We have now passed in review nearly all that is at present known of the nebulæ, so far as their appearance and form have been revealed by the largest telescopes. The information as yet furnished by the spectroscope on this subject is certainly much less extensive, but is nevertheless of the greatest importance, since the spectroscope has power to reveal the nature and constitution of these remote heavenly bodies. It must here again be remembered that the character of the spectrum not only indicates what the substance is that emits the light, but also its physical condition. If the spectrum be a *continuous* one, consisting of rays of every color or degree of refrangibility, then the source of light is either a *solid* or *liquid* incandescent body; if, on the contrary, the spectrum be composed of *bright lines* only, then it is certain that the light comes from *luminous gas;* finally, if the spectrum be continuous, but crossed by *dark* lines interrupting the colors, it is an indication that the source of light is a solid or liquid incandescent body, but that the light has passed through an atmosphere of vapors at a lower temperature, which, by their selective absorptive power, have abstracted those colored rays which they would have emitted had they been self-luminous.

When Huggins first directed his telespectroscope, in August, 1864, to one of these objects, a small but very bright nebula, he found, to his great surprise, that the spectrum, instead of being a continuous colored band, such as that given by a star, consisted only of *three bright lines.*

This one observation was sufficient to solve the long-vexed question, at least for this particular nebula, and to prove that it is not a cluster of individual, separable stars, *but is actually a gaseous nebula, a body of luminous gas.* In fact, such a spectrum could only be produced by a substance in a state of gas; the light of this nebula, therefore, was emitted neither by solid nor liquid incandescent matter, nor by gases in a state of extreme density, as may be the case in the sun and stars, but by *luminous gas in a highly rarefied condition.*

In order to discover the chemical nature of this gas, Huggins followed the usual methods of comparison, and tested the spectrum with the Fraunhofer lines of the solar spectrum, and the bright lines of terrestrial elements.

Besides the spectrum containing these three bright lines, the nebula gave also a very faint continuous spectrum, of scarcely perceptible width, which, from its nature, could proceed only from the diffused light of a faintly glowing nucleus, either solid or liquid, or from faintly luminous matter in the form of a cloud of solid or liquid particles.

All *planetary* nebulæ yield the same spectrum; the bright lines appear with considerable intensity in the spectroscope, and are of sufficient brilliancy to compare with the bright lines in the spectrum of a candle, although the nebulæ may not be brighter in the heavens than stars of the ninth magnitude. The reason of this is, that the light of the candle is spread out into a continuous spectrum, while that of the nebula remains concentrated into a few lines. The principle is identical with that by which the spectra of the solar prominences have been since observed in sunlight simultaneously with the greatly subdued spectrum of daylight.

During the years 1865 and 1866, more than sixty nebulæ were examined by Huggins with the spectroscope, mainly with the intention of ascertaining whether those which were clearly resolvable by the telescope into a cluster of bright points, gave a continuous spectrum, or one composed of bright lines.

As a result of his observations, Huggins divides the nebulæ into two groups:

1. The nebulæ giving a spectrum of one or more bright lines.
2. The nebulæ giving a spectrum apparently continuous.

About a third of the sixty nebulæ observed belong to the first group; their spectrum consists of one, two, or three bright lines; a few showing at the same time a very narrow, faint, continuous spectrum.

The great nebula of Orion (Fig. XII.) has been the subject of spectroscopic investigations. Its spectrum consists of three very conspicuous bright lines, one of which again indicates *nitrogen*, and another *hydrogen*.

Huggins has lately repeated his former observations with instruments of much greater power, and compared especially these two lines with those of the **terrestrial** gases, under circumstances which gave him a spectrum four times the length of the one he obtained in his earlier investigations. The result of these observations, continued for several nights, was to show the *complete coincidence*, even in this greatly extended spectrum of the nebular lines, with those of both gases, so that *there can be no remaining doubt as to the identity of the lines.*

Half of the nebulæ giving a *continuous* spectrum have been resolved into stars, and about a third more are probably resolvable; while of those yielding a spectrum of lines, *not one* has been certainly resolved by Lord Rosse. Considering the extreme difficulty attending investigations of this kind, there is scarcely any doubt that there is a complete accordance between the results of the telescope and spectroscope; *and therefore those nebulæ giving a continuous spectrum are clusters of actual stars,* while those giving a spectrum of bright lines must be regarded as *masses of luminous gas,* of which *nitrogen* and *hydrogen* form the chief constituents.

Comets and their Spectra.

Besides the planets, which, already cold or in process of cooling, derive their light from the incandescent sun, round which they revolve in their appointed orbits, all travelling nearly in one plane among the fixed stars in regular progress from west to east, there appear from time to time certain other wandering stars of peculiar aspect, which, from their rapid change of form and size, their fantastic contour, and their brilliant light, usually excite the greatest attention; these remarkable visitors are comets; and though their laws of motion have been well ascertained, yet their physical constitution has presented greater difficulties to astronomers than even that of the nebulæ. When they first become visible, their motion is evidently round the sun, but frequently in orbits of such great elongation as hardly to be called elliptical, travelling, besides, in all possible planes and directions — sometimes, like the planets, from west to east, sometimes in the reverse way, from east to west. Several of these extraordinary objects move in closed orbits round the sun, with a regular period of revolution; others come quite unexpectedly from the regions of space into our system, and retreat again, to be seen no more. The periodic comets are as follows: —

Comet.	Period.	Distance from the Sun.	
		Perihelion.	Aphelion.
Encke's,	3⅓ years.	289,000,000 miles.	350,000,000 miles.
Winnecke's,	5½ "	69,000,000 "	501,000,000 "
Brorsen's,	5¾ "	55,000,000 "	516,000,000 "
Biela's,	6¾ "	78,000,000 "	564,000,000 "
Faye's,	7½ "	156,000,000 "	543,000,000 "
Halley's,	76⅙ "	52,000,000 "	3,175,000,000 "

While these comets have but a short period, there are others, such as the comets of 1858, 1811, and 1844, the calculated periods of which amount respectively to 2,100, 3,000, and 100,000 years. Differences of quite a proportionate magnitude are observable, in relation to the points of nearest approach to and greatest distance from the sun. Encke's comet is twelve times nearer the sun at its perihelion than at its aphelion. Some of them, with an orbit extending beyond Jupiter, approach so close to the sun as almost to graze the surface. Newton estimated that the comet of 1680 came so near to the sun, that its temperature must have exceeded by two thousand times that of melted iron. At its nearest approach it was removed from the sun by only a sixth of his diameter. The comet of 1843, also, was so near the sun at its perihelion as to be seen in broad daylight.

Most comets exhibit a planetary disk, more or less bright, which is called the nucleus, and this is surrounded by a fainter cloudy or nebulous envelope, the coma; the nucleus and coma form the head of the comet. In almost all comets visible to the naked eye, there streams out from the head a fan of light — the tail, consisting of one or more luminous streaks, which vary in width and length, are sometimes straight, sometimes curved, but almost always turned away from the sun, forming the prolongation of a straight line connecting the sun and the comet. While telescopic comets are usually without a tail, which causes them to assume the appearance of a more or less irregularly shaped nebula, possessing a nucleus, an example of which is given in Donati's comet, as it appeared when first seen on the 2d of June, 1858, the comet of July, 1861, exhibited two tails, and the comet of 1844 had even six.

Comets are transparent in every part, and cause no refraction in the light of the stars seen through them. Bessel saw a fixed star through Halley's comet, and Struve one through Biela's comet, when distant only a few seconds from the centre of the nucleus, which passed over the star in both instances without either rendering it invisible or even perceptibly fainter; from accurate measures taken at the time, and the calculated motion of the comet, it was evident that the position of the star had not been changed by any refraction of the light.

Similar observations were made with respect to Donati's comet of 1858, and the comet of July, 1861. Close to the head of the former, where the tail at its commencement was about 54,000 miles in thickness, Arcturus was seen to shine with undiminished brightness; while in both comets a number of fixed stars appeared in full brilliancy through even a much thicker portion of the tail. The comet of 1828 possessed a nucleus about 528,000 miles in diameter, and yet Struve saw a star of the eleventh magnitude through it — a fact which seems to justify the conclusion of Babinet, drawn from his own observations, that a comet has no influence upon the light of a star, and that stars of the tenth and eleventh magnitude, and some even fainter, may be seen through their greatest mass, without losing in the smallest degree either their light or their color.

The tail is a prolongation of the coma, and is in most cases turned away from the sun, whether the comet be approaching or receding from the sun in the course of its orbit.

As a comet approaches the sun, the tail regularly increases, from which it appears that the sun, whether by the action of heat or other means, contributes essentially to the formation of the tail, and produces a separation of material particles from the head of the comet. The length of the tail is rarely less than 500,000 miles, and in some cases it extends as far as 100,000,000 or 150,000,000 miles. The breadth of the tail of the great comet of 1811, at its widest part, was nearly 14,000,000 miles, the length 116,000,000; and that of the second comet of the same year even 140,000,000 miles. And yet the formation of the tail takes place in a very short space of time, often in a few weeks, or even days.

The influence exercised on the formation of the tail by its approach to the sun was shown in the comet of 1680, for at its perihelion it travelled at the rate of 1,216,800 miles in an hour, and, as a consequence, put forth a tail in two days 54,000,000 miles in length.

It is easily conceivable that, under such circumstances, the mass of a comet must be exceedingly small. It is very probable that our earth actually passed, on the 30th of June, 1861, through part of the tail of the magnificent comet called the July comet, which suddenly appeared in the heavens, as if by magic, on the 29th of June, and no indication of such a contact was evinced, beyond a peculiar phosphorescence in the atmosphere, which was noticed by Mr. Hind, and also at the Liverpool Observatory. In the same way, the comet of 1776 passed among the satellites of Jupiter without disturbing their position in the slightest degree. This was not the case, however, with the comet, for the influence of the planet was so great on its small mass as to send it quite out of its course, into an entirely new orbit, which it now accomplishes in about twenty years.

We must now consider the remarkable phenomenon of a comet being divided into two parts, each part becoming a separate comet, and pursuing an orbit of its own. Such an occurrence happened to Biela's comet while under observation in the year 1845. When observed on the 26th of November of that year, it appeared as a faint nebulous spot, not perfectly round, with an increased density towards the middle. On the 19th of December it was rather more elongated, and ten days later it had become divided into two separate, cloudy masses of equal dimensions, each furnished with a nucleus and tail, and for three months one followed the other at a distance of one tenth, subsequently one fifth, of the moon's diameter. The pair made their appearance again in August, 1852, after having travelled together in one common orbit round the sun for more than six years and a half; but the distance between them had much increased, and from 154,000 miles, it had now reached 1,404,000 miles. Nor is this all: in conformity with its known period, the return of this comet was expected in the year 1859, and again in 1866, when it must have been visible from the earth, as its path crossed the earth's orbit at the place where the earth was on the 30th of November. Notwithstanding the most diligent search, however, the comet could not be found, and it would seem that either, like Lexell's comet, it has been drawn out of its orbit by some member of the solar system, or else, as analogy suggests, it has ceased to be a comet, and has passed into some other form of existence.

We must enter a little further than might seem needful for our purpose into the important phenomena observed in comets, partly by the naked eye, but more especially by the telescope, in order to obtain some ground for answering queries as to the physical nature of these heavenly bodies, as well as to acquire a standard by which to compare the facts collected

SPECTRUM ANALYSIS DISCOVERIES.

by telescopic observation with those gathered by spectrum analysis.

These questions are directed, in the first place, to the consideration of whether comets, like fixed stars and nebulæ, are self-luminous, or whether, like planets, they shine by the reflected light of the sun; in the second place, to the consideration of their material composition and physical constitution. That the nucleus of a comet cannot be in itself a dark and solid body, such as the planets are, is proved by its great transparency; but this does not preclude the possibility of its consisting of innumerable solid particles, separated one from another, which, when illuminated by the sun, give by the reflection of the solar light the impression of a homogeneous mass. It has therefore been concluded that comets are either composed of a substance which, like gas in a state of extreme rarefaction, is perfectly transparent, or of small, solid particles, individually separated by intervening spaces, through which the light of a star can pass without obstruction, and which, held together by mutual attraction, as well as by gravitation towards a central denser conglomeration, moves through space like a cloud of dust. It is not impossible that comets without a nucleus are masses of gas at a white heat, of similar constitution to the nebulæ, while those possessing a nucleus are composed of disengaged solid particles. In any case, the connection lately noticed by Schiaparelli between comets and meteor showers seems to necessitate the supposition that in many comets a similar aggregation of particles exists.

Donati, at Florence, was the first to examine spectroscopically the light of comets: he compared the spectrum of the comet I., 1864, with the spectra of metals, in which the dark places were wider than the luminous parts, and he found that the entire spectrum consisted of three bright lines.

Tempel's comet was observed in January, 1866, by Secchi and Huggins, who found that it yielded a continuous spectrum exceedingly faint at the two ends, in which three bright lines were seen by the former observer, and only one by Huggins. It appears from this, that the nucleus is at least *partially self-luminous*, and is composed of *gas in a luminous condition*. On the other hand, the continuous spectrum proves that some of the light is reflected sunlight, for it cannot be admitted that the coma is formed of incandescent solid or liquid particles.

The spectroscope gives no information as to the nature or condition of a substance from which we receive only reflected light; it is, however, probable that the coma and tail are of the same substance as the nucleus. These observations, therefore, yield no further result than that a gas in a state of luminosity is present in the comet, but that, at the same time, either from this gas or from other portions of the comet which are non-luminous, sunlight is also reflected.

Secchi's observations have been completely confirmed by those of Huggins. The spectrum of the comet consisted of three broad, bright bands, which were sharply defined at the edge towards the red, but faded away gradually on the opposite side.

It would be premature to draw decisive results from these comprehensive but as yet isolated observations. The spectrum of the three bright bands is derived unquestionably from the light of the comet's nucleus, and not from that of the coma, which is far too faint and ill-defined to produce such a spectrum; it may therefore be assumed that the nucleus is self-luminous, and that it is very possibly composed of glowing gas containing carbon.

By collating these various phenomena, the conviction can scarcely be resisted that the nuclei of comets not only emit their own light, *which is that of a glowing gas*, but also, together with the coma and the tail, reflect the light of the sun. There seems, therefore, nothing to contradict the theory that the mass of a comet may be composed of minute solid bodies, kept apart one from another in the same way as the infinitesimal particles forming a cloud of dust or smoke are held loosely together, and that as the comet approaches the sun, the most easily fusible constituents of these small bodies become wholly or partially vaporized, and, in a condition of white heat, overtake the remaining solid particles, and surround the nucleus in a *self-luminous* cloud of glowing vapor. Spectrum analysis will not be able to afford any more certain evidence regarding the physical nature of comets until the appearance of a really brilliant comet, which can be examined in the various phases it may present.

It would lead us too far from our purpose, were we to describe more minutely the extremely interesting phenomena which the telescope has revealed of the separation of cometic matter, and the gradual formation of the coma and tail; nor can we enter more fully here into the causes of the changes produced in the form of a comet by its approach to the sun, or to one of the larger planets; but we cannot pass over the extremely ingenious hypothesis brought forward by Professor Tyndall, before the Philosophical Society of Cambridge, on the 8th of March, 1869. This admirable investigator had already proved, by a series of interesting experiments, that concentrated solar light, or the electric light, decomposes the volatile vapors of many liquids, producing almost instantly a precipitate of cloudy matter, in which some very peculiar phenomena of light are displayed. The quantity of vapor may be so small as to escape detection, but the concentrated light falling upon it soon forms a blue cloud from the moving atoms of vapor which now become visible, and appear, according to the nature of the vapor, in a variety of forms, as precipitations of matter on the beams of light.

It is very striking, in this experiment, to see the astonishing amount of light that an infinitesimal amount of decomposable vapor is able to reflect. When the electric light is admitted into the tube, nothing is to be seen for the first moment; but soon a blue cloud shows itself, which is formed of almost infinitely small particles, either of vapor, or, what is more probable, of the molecules set free by its decomposition, and after some minutes the whole tube is filled with this blue color. The vaporous particles gradually augment in magnitude, and after some time (from ten to fifteen minutes) a dense white cloud fills the tube, which discharges so great a body of light that it is scarcely conceivable how so small a quantity of matter can possibly reflect so much light.

"Nothing," says Tyndall, " could more perfectly illustrate that 'spiritual texture' which Sir John Herschel ascribes to a comet, than these actinic clouds. Indeed, the experiments prove that matter of almost infinite tenuity is competent to shed forth light far more intense than that of the tails of comets."

Falling Stars, Meteor Showers, Balls of Fire, and their Spectra.

Whoever has observed the heavens on a clear night with some amount of attention and patience, cannot fail to have noticed the phenomenon of a falling star, one of those well-known fiery meteors which suddenly blaze forth in any quarter of the heavens, descend towards the earth, generally with great rapidity, in either a vertical or slanting direction, and disappear after a few seconds at a higher or lower altitude. As a rule, falling stars can only be seen of an evening, or at night, owing to the great brightness of daylight; but many instances have occurred in which their brilliancy has been so great as to render them visible in the daytime, as well when the sky was overcast as when it was perfectly cloudless. It has been calculated that the average number of these meteors passing through the earth's atmosphere, and sufficiently bright to be seen at night with the naked eye, is not less than seven million and a half during the space of twenty-four hours; and this number must be increased to *four hundred million*, if those be included which a telescope would reveal. In many nights, however, the number of these meteors is so great, that they pass over the heavens like flakes of snow, and for several hours are too numerous to be counted. Early in the morning of the 12th of November, 1799, Humboldt and Bonpland saw before sunrise, when on the coast of Mexico, thousands of meteors during the space of four hours, most of which left a track behind them of from 5° to 10° in length; they mostly disappeared without any display of sparks, but some seemed to burst, and others, again, had a nucleus as bright as Jupiter, which emitted sparks. On the 12th of November, 1833, there fell another shower of meteors, in which, according to Arago's estimation, two hundred and forty thousand passed over the heavens, as seen from the place of observation, in three hours.

Only in very rare instances do these fiery substances fall upon the surface of the earth; when they do, they are called balls of fire; and occasionally they reach the earth before they are completely burnt out or evaporated; they are then termed meteoric stones, aerolites, or meteoric iron. They are also divided into accidental meteors and meteoric showers, according as to whether they traverse the heavens in every direction at random, or appear in great numbers following a common path, thus indicating that they are parts of a great whole.

It is now generally received, and placed almost beyond doubt by the recent observations of Schiaparelli, Le Verrier, Weiss, and others, that these meteors, for the most part small, but weighing occasionally many tons, are fragmentary masses, revolving, like the planets, round the sun, which in their course approach the earth, and, drawn by its attraction into our atmosphere, are set on fire *by the heat generated through the resistance offered by the compressed air.*

The chemical analysis of those meteors which have fallen to the earth in a half-burnt condition in the form of meteoric stones, proves that they are composed only of terrestrial elements, which present a form and combination commonly met with in our planet. Their chief constituent is metallic iron, mixed with various silicious compounds; in combination with iron, nickel is always found, and sometimes also cobalt, copper, tin, and chromium; among the silicates, olivine is especially worthy of remark as a mineral very abundant in volcanic rocks, as also augite. There have also been found in the meteoric stones hitherto examined, oxygen, hydrogen, sulphur, phosphorus, carbon, aluminium, magnesium, calcium, sodium, potassium, manganese, titanium, lead, lithium, and strontium.

The height at which meteors appear is very various, and ranges chiefly between the limits of forty-six and ninety-two miles. The mean may be taken at sixty-six miles. The speed at which they travel is also various, generally about half as fast again as that of the earth's motion round the sun, or about twenty-six miles in a second: the maximum and minimum differ greatly from this amount, the velocity of some meteors being estimated at fourteen miles, and that of others at one hundred and seven miles in a second.

When a dark meteorite of this kind, having a velocity of one thousand six hundred and sixty miles per minute, encounters the earth, flying through space at a mean rate of one thousand one hundred and forty miles per minute, and when through the earth's attraction its velocity is further increased two hundred and thirty miles per minute, this body meets with such a degree of resistance, even in the highest and most rarefied state of our atmosphere, that it is impeded in its course, and loses in a very short time a considerable part of its momentum. By this encounter there follows a result common to all bodies which, while in motion, suddenly experience a check. When a wheel revolves very rapidly, the axletree or the drag which is placed under the wheel is made red hot by the friction. When a cannon ball strikes suddenly with great velocity against a plate of iron, which constantly happens at target practice, a spark is seen to flash from the ball, even in daylight; under similar circumstances, a lead bullet becomes partially melted. The heat of a body consists in the *vibratory motion of its smallest particles;* an increase of this molecular motion is synonymous with a higher temperature; a lessening of this vibration is termed decreasing heat, or the process of cooling. Now, if a body in motion — as, for instance, a cannon ball — strike against an iron plate, or a meteorite against the earth's atmosphere, in proportion as the motion of the body diminishes, and the external action of the moving mass becomes annihilated by the pressure of the opposing medium upon the foremost molecules, the vibration of these particles increases; this motion is immediately communicated to the rest of the mass, and by the acceleration of this vibration through all the particles, the temperature of the body is raised. This phenomenon, which always takes place when the motion of a body is interrupted, is designated by the expression *the conversion of the motion of the mass into molecular action or heat;* it is a law without exception, that where the *external* motion of the mass is diminished, an inner action among its particles, or heat, is set up in its place as an equivalent, and it may be easily supposed that even in the highest and most rarefied strata of the earth's atmosphere, the velocity of the meteorite would be rapidly diminished by its opposing action, so that, shortly after entering our atmosphere, the vibration of the inner particles would become accelerated to such a degree as to raise them to a white heat, when they would either become partially fused, or, if the meteorite were sufficiently small, it would be dissipated into vapor, and leave a luminous track behind it of glowing gas.

Haidinger, in a theory embracing all the phenomena of meteorites, explains the formation of a ball of fire round the meteor by supposing that the meteorite, in consequence of its rapid motion through the atmosphere, presses the air before it till it becomes luminous. The compressed air in which the solid particles of the surface of the meteorite glow then rushes on all sides, but especially over the surface of the meteor behind it, where it encloses a pear-shaped vacuum which has been left by the meteorite, and so appears to the observer as a ball of fire. If several bodies enter the earth's atmosphere in this way at the same time, the largest among them precedes the others, because the air offers the least resistance to its proportionately smallest surface; the rest follow in the track of the first meteor, which is the only one surrounded by a ball of fire. When, by the resistance of the air, the motion of the meteor is arrested, it remains for a moment perfectly still; the ball of fire is extinguished, the surrounding air rushes suddenly into the vacuum behind the meteor, which, left solely to the action of gravitation, falls vertically to the earth. The loud, detonating noise usually accompanying this phenomenon finds an easy explanation in the violent concussion of the air behind the meteor, while the generally received theory that the detonating noise is the result of an explosion or bursting of the meteorite, does not meet with any confirmation.

The circumstance that most meteors are extinguished before reaching the earth seems to show that their mass is but small; but this is not always the case. If the distance of a meteor from the earth be ascertained, as well as its apparent brightness as compared with that of a planet, it is possible, by comparing its luminosity with that of a known quantity of ignited gas, to estimate the degree of heat evolved in the meteor's combustion. As this heat originates from the motion of the meteor being impeded or interrupted by the resistance of the air, and as this motion or momentum is exclusively dependent on the speed of the meteor, as well as upon its mass, it is possible, when the rate of motion has been ascertained by direct observation, to determine the mass. Professor Alexander Herschel has calculated, by this means, that those meteors of the 9th and 10th of August, 1863, which equalled the brilliancy of Venus and Jupiter, must have possessed a mass of from five to eight pounds, while those which were only as bright as stars of the second or third magnitude would not be more than about ninety grains in weight. As the greater number of meteors are less bright than stars of the second magnitude, the faint meteors must weigh only a few grains; for according to Professor Herschel's computation, the five meteors observed on the 12th of November, 1865, some of which surpassed in brilliancy stars of the first magnitude, had not an average weight of more than five grains; and Schiaparelli estimated the weight of a meteor from other phenomena to be about fifteen grains. The mass, however, of the meteoric stones which fall to the earth is considerably greater, whether they consist of one single piece, such as the celebrated iron-stone discovered by Pallas in Siberia, which weighed about two thousand pounds, and the meteorites of the Mexican desert,*

---

* THE METEORITES OF THE MEXICAN DESERT. — With the object of fixing with greater precision the geographical position of the meteoric masses that have been from time to time met with on the Bolson de Mapini, Dr. J. Lawrence Smith has communicated a paper to the *American Journal of Science* for November, 1871, 335. There were already known the Cohahuila meteorite of 1854 (1), the Cohahuila meteorite of 1868 (2), the Chihuahua iron of 1854 (3), still at the *Hacienda de Conception*, and weighing about four thousand pounds, and the Tucson iron (4), found in 1854 on the north of the Rio Grande, and having the form of a ring. This mass weighs from two to three thousand pounds. A fifth mass (5) has since been heard of on the western border of the Mexican desert, that has received the name of the *San Gregario meteoric iron*. It measures six feet six inches in length, is five feet six inches high, and four feet thick at the base. On one part of its surface, 1821 has been cut with a chisel. Its weight is calculated to be about five tons. An examination of a fragment showed it to be one of the softer meteoric irons. It has a specific gravity of 7.84, and consists of ninety-five per cent. of iron, and five per cent. of nickel, inclusive of a little cobalt. Still more recently, news has arrived of the discovery, in the central portion of the desert, of a huge meteorite (6), larger than any yet found in this locality. Dr. Lawrence Smith's paper is illustrated with a little map, indicating their rel-

or of a cloud composed of many small bodies, which penetrate the earth's atmosphere in parallel paths, and which, from a simultaneous ignition and descent upon the earth, present the appearance of a large meteor bursting into several smaller pieces. Such a shower of stones, accompanied by a bright light and loud explosion, occurred at L'Aigle, in Normandy, on the 26th of April, 1803, when the number of stones found in a space of fourteen square miles exceeded two thousand. In the meteoric shower that fell at Kuyahinga, in Hungary, on the 9th of June, 1866, the principal stone weighed about eight hundred pounds, and was accompanied by about a thousand smaller stones, which were strewed over an area of nine miles in length by three and one quarter broad.

It must not be supposed, however, that the density of such a cosmical cloud is as great, when out of the reach of the attraction of the sun and the earth, as when its constituents fall upon the earth's surface. Schiaparelli calculates, from the number of meteors observed yearly in the month of August, that the distance between any two must amount, on the average, to four hundred and sixty miles. As the cosmical clouds which produce the meteors approach the sun in their wanderings from the far-off regions of space, they increase in density some million times; therefore the distance between any two meteors, only a few grains in weight, before the cloud begins to be condensed, may be upwards of forty thousand miles.

The most striking example of such a cosmical cloud, composed of small bodies loosely hung together, and existing

---

ative positions. He believes they are the result of two falls. The Tucson iron has characters that distinguish it from the remaining five. The latter, he considers, fell at an epoch probably far remote, moving from north-west to south-west during their descent. 1 and 2 fell first, 85 miles apart. The distances between the larger masses are,—from 2 to 6, 135 miles; from 6 to 5, 165 miles; and from 5 to 3, about 90 miles with hardly any connection one with another, is exhibited in the meteoric showers occurring periodically in August and November. It is an ascertained fact that, on certain nights in the year, the number of meteors is extraordinarily great, and that at these times they shoot out from certain fixed points in the heavens. The shower of meteors which happens every year on the night of the 10th of August, proceeding from the constellation of Perseus, is mentioned in many old writings. The shower of the 12th and 13th of November occurs periodically every thirty-three years, for three years in succession, with diminishing numbers; it was this shower that Alexander Von Humboldt and Bonpland observed on the 12th of November, 1799, as a real rain of fire. It recurred on the 12th of November, 1833, in such force that Arago compared it to a fall of snow, and was lately observed again in its customary splendor in North America, on the 14th of November, 1867. Besides these two principal showers, there are almost a hundred others, recurring at regular intervals; each of these is a cosmical cloud, composed of small, dark bodies, very loosely held together, like the particles of a sand cloud, which circulate round the sun in one common orbit. The orbits of these meteor streams are very diverse; they do not lie approximately in one plane, like those of the planets, but cross the plane of the earth's orbit at widely different angles. The motion of the individual meteors ensues in the same direction in one and the same orbit; but this direction is in some orbits in conformity with that of the earth and planets, while in others it is in the reverse order.

The earth, in its revolution round the sun, occupies every day a different place in the universe; if, therefore, a meteoric shower pass through our atmosphere at regular intervals, there must be at the place where the earth is at that time an accumulation of these small cosmical bodies, which, attracted by the earth, penetrate its atmosphere, are ignited by the resistance of the air, and become visible as falling stars. A cosmical cloud, however, cannot remain at a fixed spot in our solar system, but must circulate round the sun as planets and comets do; whence it follows that the path of a periodic shower intersects the earth's orbit, and the earth must either be passing through the cloud, or else very near to it, when the meteors are visible to us.

The meteor shower of the 10th of August, the radiant point of which is situated in the constellation of Perseus, takes place nearly every year, with varying splendor; we may therefore conclude that the small meteors composing this group form a ring round the sun, and the earth every 10th of August is at the spot where this ring intersects our orbit; also that the ring of meteors is not equally dense in all parts: here and there these small bodies must be very thinly scattered, and in some places even altogether wanting.

Fig. XIX. shows a very small part of the elliptic orbit which this meteoric mass describes round the sun S. The earth encounters this orbit on the 10th of August, and goes straight through the ring of meteors. The dots along the ring indicate the small, dark meteors which ignite in our atmosphere, and are visible as shooting stars. The line m is the line of intersection of the earth's orbit and that of the meteors; the line P S shows the direction of the major axis of their orbit. This axis is fifty times greater than the mean diameter of the earth's orbit; the orbit of the meteors is inclined to that of the earth at an angle of 64° 3', and their motion is retrograde, or contrary to that of the earth.

The November shower is not observed to take place every year on the 12th or 13th of that month, but it is found that every thirty-three years an extraordinary shower occurs on those days, proceeding from a point in the constellation of Leo. The meteors composing this shower, unlike the August one, are not distributed along the whole course of their orbit, so as to form a ring entirely filled with meteoric particles, but constitute a dense cloud, of an elongated form, which completes its revolution round the sun in thirty-three years, and crosses the earth's path at that point where the earth is every 13th of November.

When the November shower reappears after the lapse of

FIG. XIX.

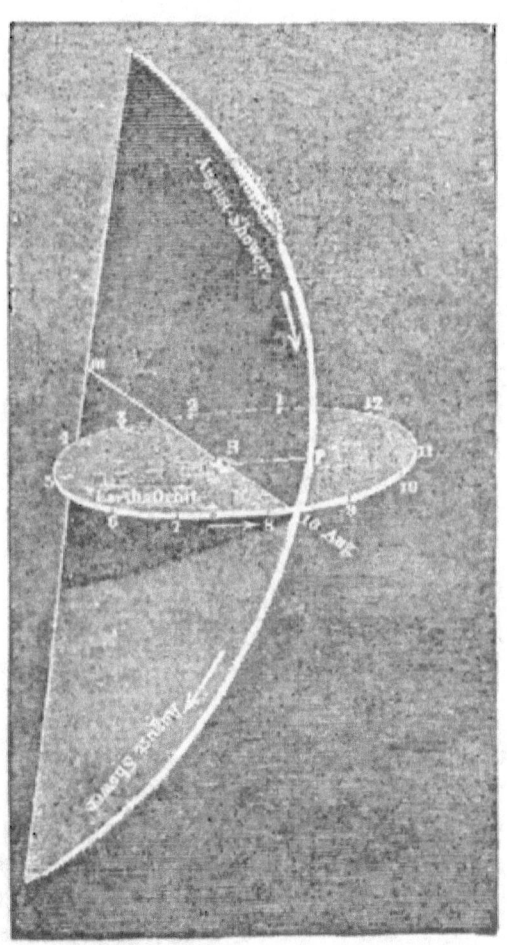

ORBIT OF THE METEOR SHOWER OF THE 10th OF AUGUST.

thirty-three years, the phenomenon is repeated during the two following years on the 13th of that month, but with diminished splendor; the meteors, therefore, extend so far along the orbit as to require three years before they have all crossed the earth's path at the place of intersection; they are, besides, unequally distributed, the preceding part being much the most dense.

A very small part of the elliptic orbit, and the distribution of the meteors during the November shower, is represented in Fig. XX. As shown in the drawing, this orbit intersects that of the earth at the place where the earth is about the 14th of November, and the motion of the meteors, which occupy only a small part of their orbit, and are very unequally distributed, is retrograde, or contrary to that of the earth. The inclination of this orbit to that of the earth is only $17° 44'$; its major axis is about ten and one third times greater than the diameter of the earth's orbit, and the period of revolution for the densest part of the meteorites round the sun S is thirty-three years three months.

From all we have now learned concerning the nature and constitution of comets, nebulæ, cosmical clouds, and meteoric swarms, an unmistakable resemblance will be remarked among these different forms in space. The affinity between comets and meteors had been already recognized by Chladni, but Schiaparelli, of Milan, was the first to take account of all the phenomena exhibited by these mysterious heavenly bodies, and with wonderful acuteness to treat successfully the mass of observations and calculations which had been contributed during the course of the last few years by Oppolzer, Peters, Bruhns, Heis, Le Verrier, and other observers. He not only shows that the orbits of meteors are quite coincident with those of comets, and *that the same object may appear to us at one time as a comet and at another as a shower of meteors*, but he proves also, by a highly elegant mathematical calculation, that the scattered cosmical masses known to us by the name of nebulæ would, if in their journey through the universe they were to come within the powerful attraction of our sun, be formed into comets, and these again into meteoric showers.

SPECTRUM ANALYSIS DISCOVERIES.

The following is a short statement of Schiaparelli's theory. Nebulæ are composed of cosmical matter, in which, as yet, there is no central point of concentration, and which has not become sufficiently dense to form a celestial body, in the ordinary sense of the term. The diffuse substance of these cosmical clouds is very loosely hung together; its particles are widely separated, thus constituting masses of enormous extent, some of which have taken a regular form, and some not. As these nebulous clouds may be supposed to have, like our sun, a motion in space, it will sometimes happen that such a cloud comes within reach of the power of attraction of our sun. The attraction acts more powerfully on the preceding part of the nebula than on the further and following portion; and the nebula, **while still at** a great distance, begins to lose its original spherical form, and becomes considerably elongated. Other portions of the nebulous mass follow continuously the preceding part, until the sphere is converted into a long cylinder, the foremost part of which, that towards the sun, is denser and more pointed than the following part, which retains a portion of its original breadth. As it nears the sun, this transformation of the nebulous cloud becomes more complete: illuminated by the sun, the preceding part appears to us as a dense nucleus, and the following part, turned away from the sun, as a long tail, **curved in consequence** of the lateral motion preserved by the nebula during its progress. Out of the original spherical nebula, quite unconnected with our solar system, a comet has been formed, which, in its altered condition, will either pass through our system, to wander again in space, or else remain as a permanent member of our planetary system. The form of the orbit in which it moves depends on the original speed of the cloud, its distance from the sun, and the direction of its motion, and thus its path may be elliptical, hyperbolical, or parabolical; in the last two cases, the comet appears only once in our system, and then returns to wander in the **realms of space**; in the former case, it abides with us, and accomplishes its course round the sun, like the planets, in a certain fixed period of years. From this it is evident that the orbits of comets may occur at every possible angle to that of the earth, and that their motion will be sometimes progressive and sometimes retrograde.

The history of the cosmical cloud does not, however, end with its transformation into a comet. Schiaparelli shows in a striking manner that, as a comet is not a solid mass, but consists of particles each possessing an independent motion, the head or nucleus nearer the sun must necessarily complete its orbit in less time than the more distant portions of the tail. The tail will therefore lag behind the nucleus in the course of the comet's revolution, and the comet, becoming more and more elongated, will at last be either partially or entirely resolved into a ring of meteors. In this way, the whole path of the comet becomes strewn with portions of its mass, — with those small, dark, meteoric bodies which, when penetrating the earth's atmosphere, become luminous, and appear as falling stars. Instead of the comet, there now revolves round the sun a broad ring of meteoric stones, which occasion the phenomena we every year observe as the August meteors. Whether this ring be continuous, and the meteoric masses strewn along the whole course of the path of the original comet, or whether the individual meteors, as in the November shower, have not filled up entirely the whole orbit, but are still partially in the form of a comet, is in the transformation of a cosmical cloud through the influence of the sun only a question of time; in course of years, the matter composing a comet which describes an orbit round the sun must be dispersed over its whole path; *if the original orbit be elliptical, an elliptic ring of meteors will gradually be formed from the substance of the comet, of the same size and form as the original orbit.*

Schiaparelli has in fact discovered so close a resemblance between the path of the August meteors and that of the comet of 1862, No. III., that there cannot be any doubt as to their complete identity. The meteors to which we owe the annual display of falling stars on the 10th of August are not distributed equally along the whole course of their orbit; it is still possible to distinguish the agglomeration of meteoric particles which originally formed the cometary nucleus from the other less dense parts of the comet; thus in the year 1862, the denser portion of this ring of meteors, through which the earth passes annually on the 10th of August, and which causes the display of falling stars, was seen in the form of a comet, with head and tail as the densest parts, approached the sun and earth in the course of that month. Oppolzer, of Vienna, calculated with great accuracy the orbit of this comet, which was visible to the naked eye. Schiaparelli had previously calculated the orbit of the meteoric ring, to which the shooting stars of the 10th of August belong before they are drawn into the earth's atmosphere. The almost perfect identity of the two orbits justifies Schiaparelli in the bold assertion that *the comet of 1862, No. III., is no other than the remains of the comet out of which the meteoric ring of the 10th of August has been formed in the course of time.* The difference between the comet's nucleus and its tail, that has now been formed into a ring, consists in that while the denser meteoric mass forming the head approaches so near the earth once in every hundred and twenty years as to be visible in the reflected light of the sun, the more widely scattered portion of the tail composing the ring remains invisible, even though the earth passes through it annually on the 10th of August. Only fragments of this ring, composed of dark meteoric particles, become visible as shooting stars when they penetrate our atmosphere by the attraction of the earth, and ignite by the compression of the air.

 A cloud of meteors of such a character can naturally only be observed as a meteor shower when in the nodes of its orbit, — that is to say, in those points where it crosses the earth's orbit, — and then only when the earth is also there at the same time, so that the meteors pass through our atmosphere. The nebula coming within the sphere of attraction

Fig. XX.

Orbits of the August and November Meteor Showers.
(Orbits of Comets III.; 1862, and I., 1866.)

of our solar system, would, at its nearest approach to the sun (perihelion), and in the neighboring portions of its orbit, appear as a *comet*, and when it grazed the earth's atmosphere would be seen as a *shower of meteors*.

Calculation shows that this ring of meteors is about ten thousand nine hundred and forty-eight millions of miles in its greatest diameter. As the meteoric shower of the 10th of August lasts about six hours, and the earth travels at the rate of eighteen miles in a second, it follows that the breadth of this ring, at the place where the earth crosses it, is four million forty-three thousand five hundred and twenty miles. In Fig. XX., A B represents a portion of the orbit of the comet of 1862, No. III., which is identical with that (Fig. XIX.) of the August shower.

The calculations of Schiaparelli, Oppolzer, Peters, and Le Verrier have also discovered the comet producing the meteors of the November shower, and have found it in the small comet of 1866, No. I., first observed by Tempel, of Marseilles. Its transformation into a ring of meteors has not proceeded nearly so far as that of the comet of 1862, No. III. Its existence is of a much more recent date; and therefore the dispersion of the meteoric particles along the orbit, and the consequent formation of the ring, is but slightly developed.

According to Le Verrier, a cosmical nebulous cloud entered our system in January 126, and passed so near the planet Uranus as to be brought by its attraction into an elliptic orbit round the sun. This orbit is the same as that of the comet discovered by Tempel, and calculated by Oppolzer, and is identical with that in which the November group of meteors make their revolution.

Since that time, this cosmical cloud, in the form of a comet, has completed fifty-two revolutions round the sun, without its existence being otherwise made known than by the loss of an immense number of its components, in the form of shooting stars, as it crossed the earth's path in each revolution, or in the month of November in every thirty-three years. It was only in its last revolution, in the year

1866, that this meteoric cloud, now forming part of our solar system, was first seen as a comet.

The orbit of this comet is much smaller than that of the August meteors, extending at the aphelion as far as the orbit of Uranus, while the perihelion is nearly as far from the sun as our earth. The comet completes its revolution in about thirty-three years and three months, and encounters the earth's orbit as it is approaching the sun towards the end of September. It is followed by a large group of small meteoric bodies, which form a very broad and long tail, through which the earth passes on the 13th of November. Those particles which come in contact with the earth, or approach so near as to be attracted into its atmosphere, become ignited, and appear as falling stars. As the earth encounters the comet's tail, or meteoric shower, for three successive years at the same place, we must conclude the comet's track to have the enormous length of seventeen hundred and seventy-two millions of miles. In Fig. XX., C D represents a portion of the orbit of this comet, which is identical with the orbit of the November meteors.

By the side of these important conclusions, which the observation and acuteness of modern astronomers have been able to make concerning the nature and mutual connection of nebulæ, comets, meteors, and balls of fire, the results of spectrum analysis, as applied to meteors, will seem to be exceedingly scant. This is easy to understand when we reflect how rapidly these fiery meteors rush through our atmosphere, and how difficult it is to lay hold of them with the spectroscope during their instantaneous apparition. Before the instrument can be directed to a meteor or ball of fire, and the focus adjusted, the object has disappeared from view. The application, therefore, of spectrum analysis to these fleeting visitors is left almost entirely to chance, and is mainly confined to those nights in which yearly, or at certain known periods, an extraordinary shower of falling stars is expected to occur.

The principal result of the investigations thus far made is confined, therefore, to the establishment of the fact that meteors consist of *incandescent solid bodies*, and that a difference is discernible in the chemical composition of the August and November meteoric showers.

The November shower of 1868 was observed by Secchi. Among the numerous meteors that left a train of light behind them, was one, the track of which lasted fifteen minutes, and was at first sufficiently bright to allow of examination by a prism. Secchi found the spectrum to be discontinuous, and the principal bright bands and lines were red, yellow, green, and blue. Besides this observation, Secchi was so fortunate as to see two meteors in the spectroscope: the magnesium line appeared with great distinctness, besides which some lines were also seen in the red.

On account of the great difficulty of observing meteors with a narrow setting of the slit, ordinary spectroscopes are not suited to this purpose. The only resource, therefore, is to substitute a cylindrical lens for the slit. There can be no doubt, however, that an apparatus will be invented which will be employed in future with great success in the investigation of meteors by means of spectrum analysis.

www.ingramcontent.com/pod-product-compliance
Lightning Source LLC
Chambersburg PA
CBHW020109170426
43199CB00009B/459